Don't Be S.A.D!

Beat Social Anxiety Disorder!

These 51 Effective Strategies Will Lead You to a More Enjoyable Work Life!

By Tony Smart

responsibility of the recipient reader. Under no circumstances will any legal responsibility or blame be held against the publisher for any reparation, damages, or monetary loss due to the information herein, either directly or indirectly.

Respective authors own all copyrights not held by the publisher.

The information herein is offered for informational purposes solely, and is universal as so. The presentation of the information is without contract or any type of guarantee assurance.

The trademarks that are used are without any consent, and the publication of the trademark is without permission or backing by the trademark owner. All trademarks and brands within this book are for clarifying purposes only and are the owned by the owners themselves, not affiliated with this document.

Table of Contents

Introduction

Most people will exhibit a natural dose of shyness or embarrassment from time to time - it's only natural. Mild shyness is also a mere personality trait for some people, as we all have varying degrees of openness to the world around us. In moderation, shyness is generally well-accepted and sometimes even appreciated.

As such, being shy has very little to do with having a social anxiety disorder (SAD), although a milder case might appear similar in the eye of an untrained outside observer. Instead of a personality trait or some adorable quirk that your friends can poke fun at in a lighthearted manner, social anxiety is a burden that lays heavily on a sufferer's mind. Since you're here, though, you are probably well aware of that difference already.

It can hardly be denied that humans are social creatures. It's not just a matter of liking to interact with others and enjoying people's company, though. Our social nature is evident in every facet of our civilization and, without it, everything would break down. Some people are certainly more sociable than others, but the truth is that getting most things done or succeeding in many areas of life will often require social interaction. This is especially true in workplaces that entail various corporate and office environments, where the focus is on teamwork and cooperative efforts.

There are many factors that can determine your performance in the workplace, your ability to climb the corporate ladder, or the amount of overall fulfillment that you get from your work. Cognitive intelligence has been used as the ultimate predictor of successful outcomes in most aspects of life, especially in professional life. As it turns out, however, other things can make us or break us in the workplace, one of which is an ability to communicate effectively, which is often regarded as an aspect of emotional intelligence.

What's also important to understand is that human beings aren't social creatures just for convenience's sake and that this nature goes much deeper than that. We have evolved to be social and to communicate, and these traits are ingrained into the very core of our being. It is, therefore, hardly any surprise that prolonged isolation has been known to have devastating effects on people's mental health. This is why problems like social anxiety are so tragic and worthy of our attention.

Being a disorder that makes social interaction difficult and sometimes incredibly stressful, social anxiety is something that puts a barrier between you and your natural need to communicate. Unfortunately, social anxiety can lead to many other mental problems apart from itself. Many aspects of life depend on social interaction and skill, social anxiety will lead to a sharp, overall decrease in a person's quality of life. Social anxiety disorder doesn't just bar you from having a good time or making a friend – it prohibits you from an accomplished and fulfilling life altogether.

Social anxiety is a massive problem and it seems to be growing. On the individual level, this form of anxiety can negatively affect your motivation to pursue your goals, work, study, and be proactive in general. Generally speaking, however, the prevalence of social anxiety has far-reaching effects that concern us all, not only the unfortunate folks who are quietly suffering from this disorder.

Anxiety disorders, in the most general sense, are an ever-growing problem in the US and they are the most common form of mental disorders with around 40 million adults affected. Every year, more than 18% of Americans over the age of 18 report suffering from some form of anxiety disorder. Among the numerous different forms of anxiety, the prevalence of social anxiety comes second to diagnosed phobias at around 15 million adults affected. This means that some 7% of the adult American population suffers from at least a mild case of SAD for a more extended period. However, the percentage of those who will have at least a short-lived experience with social anxiety at some point in their lives is significantly higher.

The incidence of SAD is all but equal among men and women, with some estimates putting women slightly higher. The onset of social anxiety disorder tends to be somewhat early, beginning around 13 years of age in many cases, but it can certainly develop at other points in life. More often than not, though, SAD seems to coincide with adolescence. This is a very insidious side to the disease because adolescence is the time when we are particularly vulnerable. When it creeps its way into your mind at an early age, social anxiety can become a part of your identity and feel normal. This is perhaps one of the reasons why, as statistics have shown, many of those affected will go on for ten years before they seek help for their problem.

Anxiety disorders, SAD included, are also a significant economic burden both on the individual and on society. In the early 2000s, the annual cost of anxiety disorders in the US was estimated to be up to $47 billion, which was over 30% of all expenditures related to mental illness. Seeing as both the number of those affected and those willing to seek help is growing, that cost has likely only increased since then. The cost of social and other anxiety disorders on the economy is not just in the way of treatment and medication. Social anxiety can severely inhibit productivity, which accounts for a significant portion of those costs.

Social anxiety disorder is also often accompanied by one or more additional mental disorders, common issues like depression. As such, comorbidity is common, but the nature of the relationship between SAD and the other conditions can vary, with SAD sometimes being the cause and at other times the result of another condition.

Another common and bigger problem that sufferers with social anxiety disorder can have is substance abuse. Of course, substance abuse itself can take on the form of a mental disorder, and it usually occurs as a result of people's attempts to self-medicate. Alcohol and various drugs can provide momentary relief and make it easier to get through otherwise stressful social situations, but in the long-term, they are bound to create more problems than they will solve. Substance abuse is how social anxiety disorder can indirectly impact your family life and destroy your existing relationships. Substance abuse and your job also won't mix well.

The greatest cost of this disorder is, of course, the human cost. One way to estimate this cost is in the wasted potential in the lives of unfortunate individuals who are held down by social anxiety. Finding a new job, holding that job, building a relationship, or breaking a cycle of loneliness are all very difficult with social anxiety. Social anxiety doesn't discriminate, and it can affect people of high intelligence, ambition, and ideas, preventing them from realizing their potential.

On top of the things we just mentioned, extreme cases of social anxiety can eventually lead to total isolation and finally suicide, which is why it's important to take this problem very seriously. Luckily, there are many strategies, tips, and techniques you can use to combat this condition and get through your day, not just at work but in general.

These are proven strategies based upon decades of research, and they will be condensed into this guide for easy reading. You will find that the techniques are presented in simple language designed to give you quick results and equip you with the mental tools to help you in your everyday life at work and elsewhere. This means that many of the strategies we present will relate to workplaces, but a lot of the knowledge is undoubtedly universally applicable and you will find that it can help in other stressful, social situations.

For over thirty years, I have worked with many people throughout many companies and international organizations, at all levels. During this time, I have mentored hundreds of employees who have struggled with social anxiety. I have taught them how to manage their condition on a day to day basis. Helping social anxiety sufferers and seeing the positive results in their lives has always brought immense happiness to me.

The techniques I have used are the ones that now lay before you, and you will find that they will significantly help you, at the very least, learn how to manage the condition well. My decades' worth of experience, and the knowledge that I have accumulated during that time have been translated into these pages, straightforward, easy to digest. The goal is to present you with information that makes sense, is easy to absorb, and can then easily be applied in your daily life, starting right away.

Apart from being comprehensive, another benefit of this book is that you will be able to use it to help others understand your problem as well. Sometimes, explaining the things we're going through can be challenging. Before outlining the solution, this book will also present the problem in detail, so even you might learn some new things about your condition. Not to mention, some issues tend to look less intense once we thoroughly understand them.

You can read one of these chapters a day and try applying these techniques one step at a time. You will find that introducing the techniques and life changes explained in this book will be very simple and straightforward. Eventually, your work life will improve significantly, and you will have a much easier time delivering presentations, going through job interviews and living day to day.

A renewed sense of ease and confidence can do wonders for your perspective and outlook – you might even start looking forward to Mondays! All you have to do to get started is read this book and commit to implementing the steps outlined.

Your perspective and mindset are essential factors in your social anxiety, and they will be as such in your efforts to combat the problem as well. This concerns your outlook on certain things in life but also the way you perceive your disorder. The problem is that social anxiety disorder can have an early onset in adolescence, as we mentioned, which means that many sufferers have had it for years and years before deciding to try and fix the issue. This often gives social anxiety a lot of time to etch itself deep into people's minds. This could mean that fixing the problem can entail quite a bit of mental rewiring.

Many of the techniques we will cover have been designed to help you do precisely that. Keep in mind, however, that as simple and straightforward as they are, these techniques might have to be practiced and applied for a more extended period, depending on the severity of your case. You should understand that battling this problem can require a serious commitment on your part.

I will give you the techniques and the information, but you are the only person who can get yourself to apply the techniques. As long as you are ready to do that, you will find that this book will provide you with more than enough information to get you well on the way toward recovering and feeling better. In time, you will experience a dramatic shift in your mindset and the whole episode with social anxiety might end up looking like nothing but a bad dream you once had. Read on, and you will find that the solutions are right there, waiting to be applied.

Chapter One: What Actually Is Social Anxiety?

Before we get into some concrete strategies and techniques, we will take some time in this first chapter to go into more detail on what precisely social anxiety is. Social anxiety, like other forms of anxiety, has been receiving an increasing amount of attention in recent decades. This has produced a lot of research on the subject, and we now have a reasonably good idea of the causes, symptoms, risk factors, and treatment of social anxiety.

There was a time when this problem was brushed off as shyness before it came to be regarded as "social phobia," which is a term that's now generally replaced with "social anxiety disorder," SAD for short. This is the problem that we will be studying and trying to help you fix throughout this book. Like any problem, it first has to be well understood before you tackle it.

So, what is social anxiety disorder really when you get down to the basics? In the simplest possible terms, SAD is a pathological condition where social situations (or the mere prospect of upcoming social situations) can cause intense, irrational anxiety or fear, which can manifest in many ways, physical and psychological.

We'll explore the actual symptoms in more detail soon, but suffice it to say that SAD has all the markings of a phobia. As such, it's not uncommon for social anxiety to lead to avoidance as well. People with SAD will often avoid many situations for fear of going through an anxiety attack again and embarrassing themselves. The fear of public embarrassment and an obsession over how others perceive us are already significant aspects of SAD, so you can see how this can begin to resemble a trap of sorts.

In these instances, the anxiety itself becomes a source of new anxiety, creating a perpetual cycle of anxiety and avoidance. It's not uncommon at all for people with social anxiety to avoid going out, pursuing career goals, or doing other things that are important for their personal development.

It's not difficult to see how this can translate to poor performance in the workplace and an inability to assert yourself. Getting a promotion, for instance, will often depend on your personal initiative, assertiveness, ability to speak publicly and voice your opinions, et cetera. All of these activities and more tend to be the biggest nightmares and difficulties for most socially anxious sufferers.

Something else worth mentioning is that "social anxiety," specifically, can refer to any and all situations where anxiety is felt in a social setting, which doesn't always mean that there is a disorder at play. As such, "social anxiety" and "social anxiety disorder" are not necessarily synonymous, although they are often used interchangeably for convenience's sake, which is what we will do as well.

Anxiety is simply a deep sense of unease and fear, which can result from a wide range of causes, many of which can be incidental. Naturally, everyone will feel anxiety at some point, so it's not always a sign of mental illness, which social anxiety disorder certainly is. For instance, it's not uncommon to feel uneasy before a huge meeting or interview that has the potential to change the course of your life.

People will get nervous, their thoughts might race, or their palms might sweat. This is a normal and natural stress reaction, and most healthy people can handle it and push through the stress more or less unhindered. With social anxiety, however, this kind of self-control is all but non-existent. If you are overcome by such anxiety and find it difficult to get a grip on yourself, even in inconsequential social situations, then you might have a problem.

Symptoms

The symptoms of social anxiety can vary in intensity on a case-by-case basis, of course, but the symptoms are generally well-understood, so it shouldn't be too difficult to diagnose the disorder.

Let it be said, though, that even social anxiety is natural to a certain degree. A specific part of it has to do with old survival mechanisms that we still carry from the time when we lived in the wilderness and formed packs. The fear of judgment or, more precisely, of doing something wrong and being rejected or ridiculed for it, comes, in part, from that pack mentality. It was mechanisms like this that kept our ancestors from messing up and putting their entire group in jeopardy.

The modern world is filled to the brim with artificial things that fool our senses and our subconscious minds, thus eliciting reactions that don't seem to make a lot of sense at first glance. Take stress reactions, for instance, which have traditionally been another core mechanism of survival. Stress used to help us get into survival mode to subdue or evade a threat successfully.

The only problem is, however, we no longer have to dodge jaguars in the jungle or scare of a pack of hungry wolves. Nowadays, the "threat" is the prospect of your car breaking down, your boss chastising you, losing your job or not paying the bills. Our world certainly does its best to nurture all sorts of disorders in us, and when you add genetic predispositions into that mix, you get an ever-growing societal problem.

With all that said, symptoms of social anxiety are what you would expect from any other form of anxiety, except that they happen during social interactions. Your heart rate will pick up, your muscles will get tense, you might get nauseous, dizzy, lightheaded, and you might experience shortness of breath. Stress-sweating is also common during outbreaks of anxiety. Your body might get washed over by alternating sensations of cold and hot, and you might experience significant blushing. These are only some of the immediate symptoms, and they can vary from person to person, with each possibly having any or all of these symptoms.

The most signature symptom has to be that ever-present, sneaking fear of judgment and rejection. Healthy people don't have this problem, at least not to the point where it can be considered a problem to begin with. Socially anxious folks, however, have to deal with these fears every day. With social anxiety, your natural need to impress is magnified many times over and also warped. It becomes an obsession and a fear that permeates daily life and can come to define your entire experience of life.

If it's allowed to grow and take over more territory, your social anxiety will invade more and more areas of your life. It will put up more barriers for you every day, preventing you from going places and doing things. Activities that you once enjoyed might become a source of much fear and frustration. You shouldn't have to give up a good time to accommodate some troubling feelings that you can't seem to shake off.

Some additional physical symptoms that come with social anxiety include; dry mouth and throat, erratic physical and verbal reactions, incoherent speech, and an inability to maintain eye contact. When it comes to the emotional side of things, socially anxious people also tend to feel out of place all the time, never quite knowing how to participate in a group or enter into a group conversation. Excessive sensitivity and defensiveness are also often present with social anxiety. The disorder will make you think that even the slightest of criticisms is a significant attack on your person, which can lead to either just discomfort or outright conflict, again, causing problems for people in the workplace. Unchecked social anxiety will also make you more vulnerable to actual attacks and insults, which will make you weaker, and that's something that everyone can do without, especially in the contemporary corporate environment.

Effects and Diagnosis

Apart from immediate, physical symptoms and discomfort, social anxiety can have a plethora of other effects on you and your life, in general. Over time, your social anxiety disorder can lead to a severe lack of self-esteem, constant negative thought patterns, depression, and ever-deteriorating, inadequate social skillset.

This combination of factors can make you despise all sorts of human interactions. After a while, it might not even be about the fear of embarrassment or inadequacy – it might just become frustrated with your inability to communicate, which then ends up pointed at everyone you come across. People will immediately sense that you are frustrated talking to them, and in time, you will become that one guy or gal who doesn't like anybody. On the inside, you will still crave interaction and relationships, but you will completely forget how to go about it. This kind of attitude and interaction doesn't work out well in workplaces either.

Something else to note is that, in some cases, the focal point of one's social anxiety isn't even in the potential public embarrassment or humiliation per se. These things are bad enough, but many socially anxious people will be more terrified of their *showing* their illness after the embarrassing situation has happened. Since social anxiety is essentially a weakness, it tends to be a source of great shame for many sufferers. This is unfortunate because talking about it can help out a lot.

Social anxiety disorder is an illness that is well-defined and has been diagnosed for quite a while now in mainstream circles. It is taken very seriously by psychiatry across the world. The diagnosis is usually made through symptom analysis and via various questionnaires and personality tests. Many such tests also exist online and are available for free, with some of them being rather detailed, extensive, and accurate.

In general, you will find a particular set of questions permeating these tests. For instance, they will ask if you worry about being embarrassed and about what people think of you. They'll also ask if you feel anxious in certain situations and to what degree and whether or not you avoid situations to evade feelings of anxiety that you expect to arise. When you answer yes to questions like these on tests, this is rather indicative of you having social anxiety.

In an even more general sense, social anxiety can affect the course of careers and even entire lives. Social anxiety can be used as a predictor of outcomes because its effects on specific skills and traits that are necessary for career advancement are well known. Since social anxiety inhibits your ability to assert yourself seamlessly, for instance, it will be challenging to distinguish yourself and score points with your employers and upper management. Being recognized is often one of the biggest problems for socially anxious people to begin with.

When you understand what social anxiety is, it isn't too difficult to tell if you have it or not. However, the best way to be sure is still going to an expert for a full, professional diagnosis. Tell your doctor about some of the symptoms you experience in social situations and voice your suspicions about having an anxiety disorder. Your doctor will direct you to a psychiatrist or some similar expert who can help you evaluate your condition.

Of course, your psychiatrist will then recommend a therapy program or offer you a prescription. You can certainly do this on your own, so you don't have to get on the program right away, but the information you will get through this consultation will still be incredibly valuable. You will get to know if you have social anxiety disorder and to what degree. You will probably also learn which areas you need to work on the most.

As we proceed through this book and talk about the various techniques you will use to fight your social anxiety, you will see how all this personal information will fit into place. By the time you've read through this, you will probably be able to outline a detailed, highly personalized strategy and course of action.

Social Anxiety with Other Disorders

Social anxiety disorder is related to numerous other conditions in many different ways. There are some problems that almost always seem to coincide with SAD, pop up as a result, act as a precursor to SAD, or are just confused with social anxiety by people who don't know the difference. Overall, some 66% of those who are diagnosed with SAD will also have at least one more mental disorder, as well, with the most common being depression.

One illness that might check any or all three of those boxes is panic disorder. We will go into much more detail on this issue later in the book, but for now, suffice it to say that it resembles an even more extreme form of anxiety and can sometimes develop from it. Nonetheless, social anxiety disorder is not to be confused with panic disorder, and anxiety attacks are not to be confused with panic attacks. The main difference is perhaps that anxiety outbursts are always easily identifiable as only that – anxiety.

Panic attacks, on the other hand, can give you the impression that you have some other, more significant problem, such as an impending heart attack. These feelings can be so terrifying that people who experience severe panic attacks will often end up in a hospital, only to be discharged soon after that once their panic attack had passed.

Another big one that tends to follow around right behind social anxiety is substance abuse, of course. In times of desperation and loneliness, people with severe social anxiety will try everything they can to alleviate their suffering, and this can include anything from booze to hard drugs. None of these substances will provide a solution.

The best they might do is mask the problem for a short while before creating a whole new set of their own, much worse problems. Despite the dangers of these paths being common knowledge at this point, many people suffering from anxiety or depression still succumb to this pitfall. If anything, this is a testament to how bad anxiety and dread can get in today's society.

Something else that's sometimes confused with social anxiety disorder is Asperger's syndrome. The confusion arises from the fact that Asperger's is a disorder that tends to drastically impact a person's ability to speak, articulate their points, and maintain communication with other people.

People with Asperger's are also classified as being on the autism spectrum. As such, Asperger's is a developmental disorder that usually requires intricate therapeutic measures, including plenty of drugs. While Asperger's affects more than just social skills, this is the area where it overlaps quite a bit with SAD.

For one, Asperger's patients struggle with certain non-verbal aspects of social interactions, such as eye contact, facial expressions, gestures, and postures, all of which can be erratic, senseless, or exaggerated. Asperger's patients generally struggle to form and maintain relationships not only because of their social ineptness but also because they sometimes don't even bother.

Many other, non-social symptoms of Asperger's syndrome are the usual problems experienced by autistic people. Perhaps the most important difference to point out between AS and SAD is that unlike AS, social anxiety can be treated and successfully defeated. Asperger's is one of those developmental problems that begin to arise in children before they can even fully comprehend the world.

As you can see, the reason that some people associate social anxiety with Asperger's is the social ineptness that is shared. The thing is, though, that Asperger's patients don't necessarily have to be anxious about it. Certainly, they will struggle to communicate with people, but they aren't always bothered by it as part of their illness' pathology.

With that being said, these failures to communicate can often be a cause of frustration for people with Asperger's. At best, it can be said that social anxiety might arise from Asperger's, in which case it would just fall under the umbrella of this much more severe disease. And no, your social anxiety can't turn into Asperger's, which, I've found, is always an enormous relief for many a person with SAD.

Chapter Two: Increasing Confidence – And Why You Can't Fake It!

As you can probably imagine, your levels of self-confidence and self-esteem play major roles in social anxiety. People with social anxiety almost always have a confidence problem to boot. Again, these are two things that feed into each other and form a cycle. For example, it's easy to imagine how folks who aren't confident might feel anxious about social situations and the prospect of embarrassing themselves in front of others.

On the flip side, however, having social anxiety, being aware of it, and feeling unable to fight it will often diminish your self-esteem even further. Few things can devastate your self-confidence as much as feelings of helplessness and weakness can. There are many other potential causes of low self-confidence, such as trauma, various childhood events, or even genetics. The important thing to understand and internalize is that in virtually all cases, your low self-confidence is not your fault.

Confidence is an incredibly crucial personal trait that can unlock countless doors in life; at home, at work, in relationships, and elsewhere. It is something that comes from within and follows wherever you go. It's apparent to everyone without you having to explain it, and it simply radiates from inside of you. High self-esteem and confidence are in the way you talk, walk, stand, posture, laugh, think, and interact. This strength and faith in yourself propels you forward and makes you go the extra mile to succeed.

On the other hand, most of this holds true for low self-confidence as well. It comes from within and follows you around, being apparent to everyone, leaving impressions, and manifesting itself in almost everything you do. One of the worst aspects of a confidence problem is that it often interferes with a person's motivation to self-improve.

It's a significant problem because self-improvement is one of the best ways to improve self-confidence. However, if you think little of yourself, then it might be difficult for your brain to see the point in you doing anything for yourself, so you can see how the problem goes in a circle and perpetuates itself. That is unless you decide to get a move on and put an end to it. We'll soon take a closer look at some concrete tips and steps you can take to boost your confidence, but for now, keep in mind that self-improvement can and will play a significant role in that.

There's a lot more to confidence and self-esteem than just feeling comfortable and making your presence known wherever you go. Your level of self-confidence can tell the world about your history and your life just as much as it can about your character. Before you can hope to give it the much-needed boost, you first have to understand a bit more about what confidence really is, what it means when it's low, and why that happens.

The inner workings of your brain can get very strange when it comes to this type of thing, so it might take you some time and effort before you can get your confidence to a satisfactory level. It will be more than worth it, though, as your self-confidence functions as a shield and armor against all kinds of things that might otherwise upset you and knock you off the rails. Irritability and sensitivity to criticism, both of which are common traits of the socially anxious, are almost always good indicators of low self-confidence. Once you regain confidence, you will attain a degree of inner peace that's only possible when you believe and know that you're good enough.

What Low Self-Confidence Is and Why It Happens

First, let us specify what exactly low self-confidence is not. It is not mild shyness or introversion. People who are introverted or a bit shy might not go out of their way to start conversations or always volunteer for everything at work, but this isn't the same as having no confidence. For example, a shy person might not jump to volunteer for a new project at the office, but they might have no problem taking the project on if *asked* to do so.

A person with low self-confidence, on the other hand, will run from the responsibility for fear of their own perceived inadequacy or incompetence and ultimately failure. Such a person has no faith in themselves, and their lack of assertiveness stems from that faithlessness. Deep down, they might actually want to volunteer for the project, but they are *afraid* to do so. If high self-confidence acts as a shield or a support column that keeps you standing tall, then low self-confidence certainly acts as a disability.

When it comes to the causes of low self-confidence, those can be numerous and their roots might weave their way all through your life, leading far back in time. That's not always the case, though, because genes can also play a significant role in how confident we grow up to be. This has to do with your brain and how easily it can access the production of certain natural chemicals (neurotransmitters) that determine things like happiness and boost confidence, such as serotonin. So, while the production of this chemical can boost your self-esteem and make you more easy-going, certain genetic variations can limit the amount of serotonin you can access. The share that genes have in determining your confidence might be anywhere between 25 and 50%.

Furthermore, some behavior that might come across as a symptom of low self-confidence might be the natural result of your character and temperament. For example, some people are just more careful and calculated than others, so they might be less likely to engage in risk-taking and assert themselves that way, especially in unfamiliar circumstances. It just so happens that others often interpret this as a confidence matter. The truth is that being calculated and careful can be a very good thing, and it really has nothing to do with confidence.

Other significant factors that determine our level of confidence are past life experiences. Genes might play their part, but nothing will mold and shape you as much as life, and there is no doubt that low self-confidence is largely just learned. Trauma, of all sorts, is one of the biggest determiners of negative outcomes in self-confidence but other things as well. Growing up and walking around with memories and effects of abuse or PTSD from traumatic events can be an almost unbearable weight on your mind, and it can make anybody feel worthless. Getting over these types of things can be incredibly difficult, especially on your own.

If you can't get over past trauma on your own, you would benefit greatly from a highly personalized, individual counseling from a loved one or a good therapist. You can always try to think in a reassuring direction by reminding yourself that it's not your fault that you went through those traumatic events, keep your head up, and focus on your future projects and growth instead of dwelling in the past.

Of course, another important factor is the way your parents raised you. Parents are very flawed creatures, just like other people, but we don't fully realize that until well into adulthood. Parents can have their own frustrations and insecurities, which they sometimes take out on their kids by belittling them and lashing out. These things can cut deep and stay internalized forever. For a good portion of childhood, most children believe every single word that comes out of their parent's mouth. During this same time, children are like a sponge, taking in the world around them and absorbing everything they hear, especially that which their parents pass down.

There are many other factors that are well beyond our control, such as the messages we get from television, bullying, growing up different than others, et cetera. The most important takeaway message is that for a good portion of our lives, our self-image is something that's largely built by the world around us, unfortunately.

Can You Fake It 'till You Make It?

This is something that you might have already been told if you ever sought advice with friends or family members. Many people seem to think that confidence is something that can be faked and projected to deceive people. The truth is that this is impossible to do. Firstly, even if you manage to fool a couple of people here and there, this still won't solve the problems we listed above, such as being afraid of taking proactive steps and asserting yourself. Secondly, most people can see right through fake confidence, and it usually comes across as much worse than shyness or anxiety. Nobody likes a faker, and all this does is it makes you seem obnoxious and provides for awkward moments.

One of the core aspects or features of social anxiety is a lack of self-control or, more precisely, control over one's emotions. As such, it's quite clear why it would be difficult for someone with social anxiety to fake and project an image of self-confidence. Your anxious reactions in social situations aren't some decision that you consciously make. They come from within and are mostly automatic, so the only solution is to go to the source and fix it.

When socially anxious folks make decisions to appease their anxiety, they are being controlled by their emotions, particularly the fear and anxiety that they have. This goes back to the subject of avoidance and how dangerous it can be for your prospects of getting better. Each time you avoid a social situation just because the idea makes you nervous, you will have suffered a major defeat in this struggle. Instead, you have to say no to your emotional responses and get out there despite the inner pressure.

This will be you taking charge and exerting control over your emotions for once, not the other way around. And while you can't fake confidence, you can undoubtedly summon plain old courage and force yourself into the dreaded social situation.

How to Boost Your Confidence

So, how do you go about boosting your confidence? This is quite an old question, and it has received many answers throughout history. Even though it sounds like a bit of a cliché, the first step you can take toward boosting your confidence is just facing your fears, as we briefly discussed above.

Since social situations are what gives you trouble, you should actively seek them out instead of hiding. As part of your experimenting, you should try to make those social situations as inconsequential as possible. Instead of experimenting at the workplace, you should try going to a bar, a library, or a busy public park, where meeting someone won't entail much more than chit-chat.

Parks have an especially high potential for social interaction if you have a dog, for instance. Even better, you can take your pet to a dog park where all the other dog owners walk their pooches. When they come across each other with their pets, dog owners are some of the most open people out there, and these interactions are some of the easiest you can have because you already have plenty to talk about thanks to the presence of pets. You never know as you might even make a real friend this way. When it comes to meeting people, spontaneity can lead to fascinating outcomes.

Wherever you decide to go, keep in mind the importance of what you will be doing. Don't underestimate the clichés such as "face your fears" or "just get out there and do it." There is merit to these simplistic pieces of advice that people dish out, especially when you're trying to break out of your cycle of anxiety and boost your self-confidence. Of course, all of this is easier said than done. If you've been struggling with social anxiety and avoidance for a long time, suddenly breaking into interaction again will be difficult. In a way, it will be like quitting an addiction cold-turkey.

This is why it might be a better idea to take a more gradual, incremental approach if your anxieties are severe. Instead of going to a highly active location and starting a full-on conversation, you can start with certain baby steps. If your problem is severe, even simple things like asking strangers for directions or the time can be a step in the right direction. After that, the idea is to incrementally expose yourself to tougher situations and gradually work your way up. This is an excellent way to condition yourself not to be afraid of social interaction while also remaining in control and not plunging yourself head-first into the unknown.

Something to keep in mind is that one of the main reasons you feel fear and anxiety in social situations is that your brain is convinced that these situations are dangerous. There are centers in your brain that deal specifically with identifying threats and alerting the body of imminent danger by causing a fear or stress reaction. That's why this gradual exposure is a form of reconditioning and rewiring of your brain. You are primarily teaching the brain that there is nothing to be afraid of, and you should remind yourself of this consciously as well. There is no threat other than what your subconscious mind is making up.

Traditionally, exercise and workout programs have also always come highly recommended as a means of boosting one's confidence. That's especially true if you are out of shape and unhappy with yourself because of that. Being overweight, for instance, usually adds a lot to the social anxiety and can bring a person down. As such, getting in shape is high on the list of things to do to increase confidence and subsequently, your social skills.

But you don't need a weight problem to start working out or exercising. Doing just a bit of cardio every day can fill up your schedule and keep you occupied but also do wonders for your health. The better care you take of yourself, the more confident you will get. Keep in mind what we said about motivation and treating yourself poorly. You first have to honestly decide that you want to feel better and live a more fulfilled life. Once you make up your mind, good things will follow.

Something else to consider is postures and body language. This is the one aspect of image projection that's worthwhile to practice. Do not slouch and walk around the office with your eyes glued to the floor. This is one of the universal signs of insecurity and disinterest, but what's even worse is when you look at the ground while talking to someone. If eye contact is something you struggle with, try to keep your head at least up and look at something other than the floor or your shoes.

Confident people stand up straight with their shoulders pushed back, which is something you should practice. Another important thing is the handshake, especially if you are a man, but it certainly applies to women as well to an extent. Firm, confident handshakes communicate stability, comfort, and openness. Of course, you shouldn't try to crush the other person's hand, but apply a healthy degree of force to let them know you're there. If you're unsure how much force to apply, you should take a mental note from how other people do it, particularly those who you know are confident.

Overall, try to introduce as many healthy and positive changes as you can into your life. Create a healthier diet, take up exercise, cut out harmful substances and bad habits, and bring order into your life. Just as importantly, you should make sure that you are reducing the stress in your life and getting enough quality sleep. All of these things will come together to get you on a wholesome, healthy path, and you will feel much stronger for it in due time.

Finally, something that's important to remember is that the people around you are rarely as confident as you might think. Your anxiety, feelings of inadequacy, second-guessing, and other quirks of the mind are not unique – not by a long shot. People question themselves all the time, and the chances are good that the ones that scare you have a bunch of problems of their own.

We're all just humans, and everyone has their own set of problems. On top of that, remember that people are not mind-readers, and most of them aren't particularly good at reading cues either. People aren't aware of your anxiety problems 24/7. They aren't continually scanning you for weaknesses and insecurities, especially when you aren't even interacting with anyone. Most of the time, people are just minding their own business, just like you.

Chapter Three: Conversation Skills – Proven Tips

As you well know, social anxiety takes a particular toll on one's ability to converse calmly and effectively, at least in some situations. Of course, a social anxiety sufferer might be capable of talking with their mother or a close friend just fine, but once strangers or uncontrolled social situations are introduced into the mix, trouble begins. As such, your conversation skills are undoubtedly an area you should work on.

While social anxiety does affect your ability to engage in conversation, that doesn't necessarily mean that you have no conversation skills. Some folks have the skills, but their anxiety renders those skills worthless. However, many people suffering from SAD actually have no conversation skills whatsoever. This is because, as we discussed earlier, social anxiety often has an early onset at around 13 years of age.

This is troublesome because teenage years are essential in honing social skills and getting a feel for how the world of grown-ups functions. SAD-stricken teens, however, will avoid social interaction and, as a result, will miss out on developing crucial social skills, one of which is verbal communication. As you can probably imagine, this creates problems beyond just social anxiety. If someone never developed proper social skills to begin with, then they won't magically appear after their social anxiety has been cured. They might not experience anxiety symptoms anymore, but they can still have difficulties establishing contact or communicating with people. Of course, social skills, including conversation skills, are luckily something that can be practiced.

Conversation is a lot like a craft that you are trying to get better at. It doesn't matter how low your starting point is; as long as you get enough practice, you will get better at it, no matter how slowly. This is why it's important not to indulge your social anxiety. Getting better at conversation will be really difficult if you aren't doing it. It's one of those things that you can familiarize yourself with from theory, but will never master without practice.

Something that's particularly great about conversation and other forms of social interaction is that these things build confidence. If you have been struggling with social anxiety for a long time and are starved of healthy and meaningful social interaction, then every little bit of success will count a whole lot. Each successful interaction, no matter how seemingly menial it is, will feel great and leave a very pleasant taste for you. Most importantly, it will leave you craving more and also feeling more confident each time.

What's unfortunate is that we are born with a need to interact and communicate, but not with the necessary skills. This is why we have to socialize in childhood and later on to hone these skills for the future. Certainly, learning the skills will come as natural and easy for a child who is growing and developing in a healthy manner, but that doesn't mean that there is a point after which it's too late. Adults who have missed out will have a more difficult time, sure, but a human being can be socialized at any point in their life if they put in enough effort and determination.

It's also worth pointing out that some people are naturally more talkative than others. A wide range of factors come together to determine such outcomes, but people can certainly be divided up into introverts and extroverts, as we briefly mentioned earlier. Extroverts not only find conversation easy, but a lot of them enjoy it all the time, no matter how mundane the topic. You don't have to be quite at that level to be healthy since being on the introverted side is perfectly fine. Nonetheless, introversion is definitely not synonymous with social ineptness, far from it.

Small Talk

Small talk is something of a building block of social interaction, and all subsequent complex interaction depends on it. It's a great place to start practicing your conversation skills with minimal risk and effort. Besides, small talk is a beneficial skill to have if you're socially anxious because it will help you break awkwardness in most situations and break those awkward silences that we all detest so much.

Uncomfortable as they are for everyone, awkward silences can be especially difficult to deal with if your anxiety begins to emerge. This can jumble you up completely and get your mind racing with thoughts of how much the other person must be judging you, how stupid you look, et cetera, all of which are just your imagination, of course.

You should keep in mind at all times the meaning of *small* talk. Don't expect to go around making people laugh, educating them about the state of affairs in the Mexican Drug War, or making them become your best friend. If you run into your neighbor in the morning or you are at the store waiting in a queue, small talk should be restricted to the simplest of things such as the weather.

The important thing for the socially anxious you is to get this valuable practice as frequently as possible. In the absence of small talk partners, you can always approach strangers, pretending to ask for directions. It might seem like a weird idea, but it doesn't hurt anybody and the stranger will have no idea you're just practicing social interaction on them. While you're doing this, do your best to try and analyze how they are reacting so you can learn to read a few basic signs.

If you ask someone for directions and they go out of their way to explain it, and they start showing interest by asking you stuff, that might be the basis for an actual conversation, especially if you really are going somewhere and can talk about it. Trust me; people have made real friends over much less – it just happens.

In fact, if a conversation kicks off from one of these mundane interactions and you see that the person really likes you, you can even disclose the fact that you're just practicing. It could certainly provide an interesting topic of discussion. You never know; maybe the person you just met has some experience with social anxiety, too, and you just made a great friend. This is just one fictional example of the things that can arise from mere small talk. For someone with social anxiety, that would be a great trade-off, considering that these interactions carry the lowest risk of unpleasant outcomes.

As smoothly as small talk might go along its natural route, it's still a good idea to have some topics of conversation ready beforehand, just in case the exchange evolves. You should consider those topics that are universal, easy, positive or at least neutral, and allow for both sides to contribute. Weather, regular news, sports, family matters, pop culture, travel, work, and hobbies or personal interests.

All of these have great potential, but there are some that definitely don't, such as religion, politics, sexual topics, personal finances, and gloomy subjects like death or tragedies. Save for perhaps personal finances, all of these topics can start outstanding discussions among friends who already know each other quite well. You should thus save them for after you've met someone and gotten to know them a bit. Furthermore, if you stumble upon someone you deep suitable for a potential romantic relationship, don't talk to them about your past relationships – this is always a bad idea. And if the conversation somehow does go there, the last thing you want to do is talk poorly of your ex or exes. This makes a very bad first impression.

While making people laugh is one of the surest ways to their heart, it's a good idea to hold off such stunts until you've gotten the hang of the whole thing. Not that there's anything wrong with trial and error, but you should avoid disappointment where possible.

Beyond Small Talk

As someone who is, for all intents and purposes, a beginner, you should stick to the defense, so to speak. The ideal position for you would be that of the listener. Most people you meet will enjoy talking about themselves, their lives, dreams, and other things, which gives you an opportunity to entrench yourself as the listener and nudge the conversation along.

And so, when you manage to get a conversation going, don't give in to the temptation to unload on the person with story after story, but don't just nod and stare at them either. You should just let the person talk and then subtly jump in with a simple question here and there to verify details and show interest. Not only is this an excellent way to practice maintaining your focus on the conversation instead of your anxiety but you will also leave a very nice impression on most people. Most folks love a good listener, and you, being so attentive and showing interest, will make them feel special.

On the other hand, when the time comes for you to lead a conversation, there are some guidelines for that as well. When describing something in more detail, particularly a situation or some personal experience, you should use simple but descriptive language that will make it easier for your listener to project themselves into the story.

Furthermore, when trying to keep any conversation going smoothly, you want to utilize questions as much as possible and make sure that they are ones that can't be answered with just yes or no. You can use what's sometimes referred to as the five W's, including who, what, where, when, and why. Start your questions with these five, and you will always breathe some additional energy into the conversation. You can also ask for further clarification via "how" or get hypothetical with your questions.

If a conversation is going particularly well, you can always throw in some of your own input as well to keep it two-sided and engage your conversational partner even more. All while the other person is talking, you can scan the story for bits and pieces that perhaps remind you of something interesting you could say. Just make sure that you don't wholly shift focus back to you and stop listening to what the person is telling you. Most importantly, though, make sure you don't hijack or derail the entire conversation to plug yourself in. Before you speak, ask yourself if your input will benefit and advance the conversation.

After a while of practice, you'll find some additional tools and tricks that can be very useful. For instance, a good way to get mentally closer to the person you are conversing with is to strategically and somewhat sparingly use their first name. Our names are powerful sounds to us, and hearing them implies a degree of closeness and intimacy.

Also, make sure that you harness the full power of smiles when you approach people but also during the conversation. As long as you're not forcing it and overplaying your hand, it's difficult to go wrong with smiling. It's a universal signal that things are fine and pleasant for everyone.

You should also make sure that you learn as much as possible from people who at least seem to be confident and communicative. If someone you are talking to looks particularly relaxed and confident, it's not a bad idea to subtly mirror them as far things like posture, tone of voice, and gestures are concerned. As long as you are subtle, this can make things a lot more comfortable, and you might learn a whole lot you can use in the future. You have to continually absorb every bit of wisdom that you see working in practice for other people. Observe and learn everything, adopt what works.

All in all, you can use these tips to plot your own mixed approach based on the situation and what you are trying to accomplish. Just remember to take gradual steps and be patient. The important thing is that you're getting practice as frequently as possible. This won't work if you manage to strike up one short conversation before going back to isolation for another month. You have to keep at it for quite a while in order to achieve permanent results.

Additional Tips

Conversation is the main or at least most obvious way in which humans communicate, but it is not the only one. Much of our communicating is on the subtle side, consisting of signals, body language, and gestures, many of which are virtually involuntary. We are very expressive creatures, although some people who have trained themselves will purposely mask as many of their cues as possible, so they can be challenging to read. Most folks don't care about that, though, and a lot of them don't really have the best self-control, so you will be able to read them like a book if you know what to look for.

Earlier, we briefly mentioned how your own body language can project insecurity or confidence through things like posture and handshakes, but this is just one small part of the puzzle. There is a whole world out there called non-verbal communication. Non-verbal communication plays a huge, natural role in how we interact, and we are telling a whole lot through it without even knowing it half the time. Folks with social anxiety are especially prone to being body language illiterates.

Apart from what we covered earlier, you can inspect the body language of your conversational partner for clues as to how they feel about you. As a general rule of thumb, the closer and more physically open a person is to you, the higher the chances are that they like you. This is especially true when romantic interest is at play. Men and women exhibit slightly different signals, but the underlying principles are the same. The more physical a person gets with you, the more they like you. Holding your gaze for a long time is also a good sign.

Keeping a distance, crossing the arms, speaking with a tense tone, and keeping the length of responses to a minimum are all good indicators that the other person isn't too fond of the conversation. Keep in mind that doesn't mean they hate you personally. They might have their own problems; something might be troubling them, they might be in a hurry, or they themselves might be anxious and insecure.

The next tip to consider applies mostly to situations like dates or other kinds of meet-ups. This is where the environmental factor can do a lot for the continuity and smoothness of your conversations. For instance, doing something bland and regular like going for a cup of coffee or some dinner, will give you a few things to focus on other than each other. Unless you're feeling like a fountain of conversation and are excited about the unending back-and-forth exchange, you should probably meet at a place that's more dynamic. In particular, it's a great idea to partake in some activity, such as a hike or a football game. When there are things around to see and do, you will have plenty of topics to fall back on if your personal exchange gets a bit dried up.

Going back to the big picture, something else that you will want to master after a while is the art of joining a conversation out of the blue but also leaving when you feel like it, without creating any unpleasant situations. You should know how smoothly and gallantly join without being weird and making anyone uncomfortable. These skills are very advanced, though, and by the time you've mastered them, you will have already become quite adept at social interaction.

Knowing how to join a conversation can be very useful in situations such as parties, especially if you find yourself alone at one. When deciding which group to join, you will want to look for two things to give you a more natural entrance: familiar people and familiar topics. If an acquaintance or even a friend of yours is already in some group, then joining them is just a matter of saying hi to your friend. In the absence of that opportunity, though, you should listen in to see what the conversation is about.

It stands to reason that you shouldn't barge in on a conversation on a topic that you know nothing about. Once something interesting catches your ear, your next step is to get closer, listen, observe, and try to establish eye contact without being intrusive. Parties and such are usually highly active, crowded places where people are more eager to talk than usual, so it shouldn't be too difficult to move in when you see a window. You can offer someone a drink or offer your opinion in a humble, preferably humorous manner. The moment when someone from the group responds, you're in.

Leaving conversations can also be surprisingly tricky, especially with social anxiety. It just takes a bit of practice and a feel for timing, though. Three golden rules could perhaps be isolated here. Firstly, use your body language to indicate that you are trying to cut off the conversation. That means slowly increasing the distance between you and the person and at least partially turning toward the direction you want to go. The second rule is not to just cut the person off unless it's an emergency. Just wait for the first little break in the conversation, quickly summarize or confirm what was said, and excuse yourself. The third rule is to be polite but not to wait for permission. You leave when you please.

Chapter Four: How You Can Deal with Social Anxiety in Your Workplace

In this chapter and those to come, we will explore various tips and strategies on how you can make your social anxiety more manageable, tackle it, and finally beat or severely reduce it. For the time being, we will take a look at some general tips and strategies on how you can manage and cope with your social anxiety. We will emphasize your work environment, but, as a rule of thumb, if it applies to your social anxiety at work, it will probably apply elsewhere as well.

It's not just about what you can do when a situation arises at work. You must think way beyond your workplace and work hours. To beat anxiety at work, you have to introduce specific lifestyle changes, make alterations to your way of thinking, adopt new mental concepts, and overcome anxiety elsewhere in your life as well.

Managing Social Anxiety

The first step is to make your social anxiety more manageable so that it doesn't cause you additional stress that makes the condition even worse over time. The one thing that makes the workplace particularly scary for socially anxious folks is that it can feel like a trap. An anxiety attack can strike while you're at a party or at a bar, and you can always just leave these places virtually on a moment's notice and run away.

Remember, it's not that you *should* run away, but you *could,* and knowing that can help many people stay despite their anxiety. Work is different, though, because it's a place where you have to go to make money and earn a living, and you can't just cut it off. This realization itself can be a source of anxiety when an affected individual's escape options essentially boil down to going to the bathroom. And that's why it's so crucial to overcome social or any other kind of anxiety in your workplace.

First and foremost, you have to make sure that your anxiety is indeed irrational. What I mean is that, sometimes, being anxious and hating your workplace can be very justified. If everything is fine and your mind is just coming up with fears to stress you out for no reason, then yes, you have some anxiety to work on. However, if you are getting bullied or abused in some way, or if your superiors are severely mistreating you, then it's no wonder you would feel stressed out and anxious all the time. As such, one of your first steps should perhaps be to establish whether or not your anxiety stems from something real. If it does, then the thing that needs solving is that real problem, whatever it is.

Furthermore, you should never rely on any crutch to get through your day at work. For instance, we already mentioned the dangers of alcohol, but it's not just about the risk of substance abuse that's at play. Each time you use a drink to calm your anxiety, you are reaffirming it and reminding yourself that you can't handle your emotions and get a grip on yourself. Before you know it, you might find yourself always having to take a shot before any important engagement and, in due time, you are sure to stray off into alcoholism territory. The same holds for any substance that you think might solve your problem.

If you ever sought advice about your social anxiety from a layperson before, perhaps you've been told that "it's all in your head." This is undoubtedly another one of the clichés that people throw around without overthinking about them, but there is a lot of truth there, as you can see. A lot of your social anxiety is quite literally make-believe. You might have convinced yourself not just that people dislike you but also that they are continually watching and, worse yet, judging your every move.

Like other negative thoughts, this false perception of reality has become habitual in the minds of people with social anxiety. You need to dispel the illusion that the world is obsessed with you enough to judge you all the time. You are the only person who can do this and change that perception, though. The more you try to interact and talk to other people; however, the more you will see how wrong you were. There is no better way to stop thinking that people are judging you than to talk to them and befriend them.

Another good way to bring your workplace anxiety levels down is to already get some socialization before getting to work. Waking up at the last minute, quickly throwing the clothes on, and just slipping into the office in the nick of time can make your anxiety worse. You should instead try to wake up earlier and introduce some healthy activities to your morning routine.

Walking your dog is a great way to start your day, especially when you run into other dog owners and have a little chat with them. Small things like this don't seem like much, but they will mean a whole lot to someone who struggles with social situations. If you don't have a dog, you can go for a bit of a jog or take a walk to the convenience store. All these things are healthy and have the potential for social interaction. You will arrive to work fully alert, refreshed, and less moody. As such, you will handle stress much better, especially if you also get quality, regular sleep.

Coping Strategies

Strategies for coping with your anxiety usually revolve around certain simple exercises, most of which are thought exercises. It's a struggle that goes on in your mind, and it's a battle that you have to fight against yourself.

One quick and simple example of what you will have to do in your head is the relabeling of your problem and shifting your perspective toward it. Instead of seeing it as anxiety, try to convince yourself that it's excitement. When you feel an onset of anxiety coming in, try and think about it as if you are getting excited about something good. It's all about shifting some gears in your brain and trying to replace as much negativity as you can with positivity.

You should also get your mind into a place where it understands that uncomfortable situations are an unavoidable fact of life sometimes. This means that you should learn to soldier through your anxiety instead of running away and hiding. If you were about to do something you wanted to do before an anxiety outbreak befell you, you should force yourself to proceed with whatever you were doing. Try to focus on that goal as strongly as you can and don't think about the background noise coming from your anxiety. You will find that choosing to forcibly ignore your anxiety might indeed subdue it for the time being.

You should embrace your anxiety. That's not to say that you should be content living with it forever, but you should stop dwelling in the doldrums, wondering why you're so messed up, how life is unfair, et cetera. Sometimes, you have to grab the cards you were given and play that hand come what may.

Better yet, you should embrace the inherently chaotic nature of the universe and come to terms with the fact that you can't control everything in life. Unfortunately, some people have a challenging time reconciling themselves with this simple truth, and the fear of losing control thus becomes quite a problem. That fear can most definitely contribute to outbreaks of anxieties of all kinds.

What I mean here is that some people will dislike you no matter what you do. Such people can sometimes hate you, even more, each time you try to appease them. Indeed, people will sometimes hate you, others will judge you, and some others will pick on you for no reason. You can't let these things get to you because there isn't a person alive whose life is just smooth sailing 24/7. Everyone has their own set of problems, and you will get your share no matter what. If you genuinely internalize that fact and focus on being ready instead of getting frustrated, you might find that your anxious reactions can decrease dramatically. In essence, you must stop trying to control everything all the time, least of all the contents of other people's minds.

When an anxiety attack begins, you will enter a sort of wrestling match with your anxiety, fighting over your mind's focus. Your anxiety wants you to turn all of your attention inward and analyze every single thing that happens to you during your outburst of anxiety. Your hand tremors, sweating, dizziness, and erratic movements are all things that you shouldn't think about. That's easier said than done, of course, but you can do it if you give yourself something to pull your attention away, such as a task you're working on.

Breathing exercises are also a coping mechanism that many people use in a variety of stressful situations. Once we get anxious, our physical symptoms can be worsened by irregular breathing and a lack of oxygen in our system. Breathing can do two things for you in these instances: provide you crucial oxygen and give you something to think about other than your anxiety. Try to breathe slowly and deeply. Take four seconds to inhale, hold the air in for four seconds, and slowly exhale over four seconds as well. You can repeat this as many times as you have to, and you can also reduce it to three seconds if four is too long for you.

Finally, you have to adopt certain beliefs that will help you perceive your anxiety as less scary and devastating. For one, you should understand your anxiety as something natural because it stems from mechanisms that all healthy people have. It just so happens that your anxious responses are misplaced in harmless situations, but that's what they essentially are – a result of adrenaline and other things that your body and brain do to react to a perceived danger.

While it might sound like a cliché, you do need to stop thinking negatively about things, especially when you have no real reason to do so. An anxious mind will find a million potential ways that some upcoming event can turn disastrous, even if that event is something you've been looking forward to for a long time. These thoughts are virtually never grounded in hard facts and are instead paranoid exaggerations. You need to make a conscious effort to break the habit of thinking this way. Either focus on the positive aspects of an upcoming engagement or find something else to think about.

Further Tips

There are countless other tips to help you relax more and bring your workplace social anxiety under control. For instance, as someone with social anxiety, you will always benefit greatly from being liked, as the opposite will make things infinitely more difficult for you.

A great way to be liked in an office environment is to be honest and consistently scrupulous. You should avoid getting involved in petty drama among your colleagues, and you most certainly shouldn't partake in spreading gossip and talking behind people's backs. Don't even nod when others talk poorly of people in front of you. You should either change the subject or find a way to get out of the picture.

Without being pushy or a nuisance, you should try and at least know everybody's name, unless your work environment makes that impossible, of course. Taking a healthy and friendly interest will score points with most people, and if you can be on friendly terms with everyone at the office, this will only be beneficial.

On top of that, it's not just about establishing friendly relationships. It's also about creating a familiar environment for yourself since familiarity is usually a great enemy of anxiety. You should especially strive for this if interacting with strangers is something you struggle with the most. When people approach you at work for whatever reason, it helps to know at least their name and their job position at the workplace.

It's not just about the comfort of familiarity, either. This information gives you something to think about and focus on while talking to a person. It allows you to focus on and think about Jim from accounting and what he is saying to you, instead of obsessing over the potential to embarrass yourself in front of a stranger, who might be from management for all you know. This is just one example of how familiarity dispels worry and gives your mind less room to experiment with dreadful thoughts.

Another tip is not to avoid asking for help when you need it. Such instances are valuable opportunities for meaningful interaction. The idea of asking for help from a superior is most likely much more uncomfortable in your mind than it will be in practice. Not only will you get to exercise some social interaction, but you will also communicate with your boss that you care about the quality of your work.

You can also ask for support with your social anxiety itself. It depends on the kind of working environment you're in and the sort of relationship that you have with your manager. If they are experienced and have been with the company for a longer time, then it's likely that they have already dealt with anxious employees. As such, your manager or boss might have some very useful tips on what you can do to function better at your job.

You should strive to keep the amount of stress you experience at your job to a minimum. An excellent way to do this is not to overburden yourself and get into situations where you will struggle. Wanting to impress our superiors, we can sometimes voluntarily get in over our heads with projects and responsibilities. Once the going gets tough, the prospect of failure can make your anxiety a whole lot worse.

You also need to foster the idea that you are not alone in your problem and that your social anxiety is not uniquely unbearable. A great way to do this is to seek out people who have the same problem if you don't know any such folks already. Your best bet is support groups for anxiety and similar problems, where you can talk to similar people and compare your stories.

All of this will facilitate an exchange of ideas, useful feedback, support, and useful programs. For instance, some support groups might give their participants small tasks or goals that they should complete. These can include starting a conversation, making a friend, or going to certain places. Whatever it is, your support group will also make you accountable and give you greater motivation to do these things. After all, it's sometimes easier to do things for others than for ourselves.

Finally, perhaps one of the best tips is to use the things you've learned about earlier and change your life *outside* of work. Indeed, many times your situation at work is a reflection and is full of symptoms of problems elsewhere in your life. Maybe you should forget about your workplace anxiety for a while, focus on exercise and a healthy diet to give your life a sense of purpose that you can think about. Furthermore, set goals for yourself in your after-work hours. Make it your mission to make at least one friend in the next two months or so and exercise your small talk and other social skills as frequently as you can to make it happen.

Chapter Five: Surviving and Thriving in Specific Workplace Situations

The general tips you have received thus far should provide you with a solid foundation on which to build your approach. Most of the stuff we have covered applies universally, and you will find that a lot of the uncomfortable situations you go through can be alleviated by adhering to those principles. In this chapter, however, we will get a bit more specific and look at some distinct situations in professional environments that sufferers of social anxiety tend to struggle with.

Each individual will struggle with these situations in their own way and to a different degree. There are no universal rules that determine which situations are the most difficult across the board.

Meetings

Statistically speaking, most cases of social anxiety tend to intensify in some situations more than in others. Meetings are perhaps not among the most challenging social situations out there. This is because they tend to involve numerous people talking to each other. Apart from the person leading the meeting, the rest of the participants generally receive the same amount of attention unless they are singled out. So a meeting is one of those situations where folks with social anxiety can stick to the sidelines and avoid drawing attention.

If meetings are something you regularly go through, then you are guaranteed to be familiar with the situation and the feeling. You get in a meeting, sit down where you believe you'll draw the least amount of attention, and you stay quiet, praying for it to be over quick. And that is undoubtedly one of the ways to "survive" through a meeting, although it does nothing except allow you to avoid a bit of discomfort while indulging your disorder.

Needless to mention, corporate meetings and other similar occasions in business environments are opportunities to distinguish yourself, assert ideas, and score points with your superiors. And so, while sticking to the sidelines and keeping to yourself might be a way to get through the ordeal, you definitely won't thrive.

One of the biggest mistakes that socially anxious folks make when it comes to meetings is not to show up too early. You might think it makes sense as part of your avoidance to show up at the last minute and avoid having to interact with other people while waiting for the meeting to start. After all, once the meeting is underway, and your boss or manager takes over, the room's attention will be on them, and you'll be "safe." This is, however, the wrong way to look at it.

The small talk and other casual interactions that occur before the meeting officially starts are a great way for you to get into character gradually, so to speak, and ease into the meeting. If you barge in at the last minute or, even worse, show up late, you will draw much more attention and make things worse. The same applies to any team effort and assignments. When you are called upon to get on a task with other people, you want to show up as early as possible to secure your place in one of the groups ahead of time.

Work meetings are situations where assertive folks can truly shine, so a little assertiveness goes a long way and is something you should practice. We'll take a more detailed look at assertiveness a bit later, but let's say that it's something that will come as you beat back your anxiety and become more confident. Even if you're not particularly assertive, there are still some ways for you to cope and perform better at meetings.

If you want to get in on the group discussion and make a contribution, remember what we talked about earlier when it comes to conversations. You should practice your conversation joining skills as well as your storytelling as these two things tend to be the most useful in meetings. Assuming you're not hiding in plain sight on the sidelines, you will have to either join the conversation or speak in front of others if asked something.

In any case, there should be at least one or two people you know, since it's a meeting at your workplace. If that's true, you should focus mostly on them because they are familiar. You will know more about the way they think and how they generally interact with you, so there will be less room for your mind to speculate about negative scenarios. As always, you should also do your best to stay focused on what you're saying, not on how others are reacting to it in their minds.

Besides, it's unlikely that you will have to share anything particularly personal or to compromise even if asked to answer questions during a group meeting. More often than not, speaking in such meetings involves either the reading of data and facts or making suggestions and expressing work-related ideas.

Something you should remember is that being aware of your strengths and weaknesses is a mark of confidence and self-acceptance. Eloquence, for instance, is a skill and strength that most people don't possess. It is not expected of you to be a brilliant orator and impress everyone with your genius, so keep it simple and don't fret. Deliver your points succinctly and clearly, and you'll be fine.

Keep in mind that your ultimate objective is to thrive, not just survive. Don't limit yourself to just learning how to answer when asked a question quickly. Practice your conversation skills as much as you can and learn how to be an active participant in meetings. Company meetings aren't a life-threatening ordeal, so everyone can "survive" them, but it takes skill to shine and score points with your superiors.

Interviews

The dreaded job interviews are far more difficult than work meetings. This is because job interviews check quite a few boxes when it comes to things that tend to trigger an outburst of social anxiety. For one, the very purpose of the interview is for you to be evaluated and judged, and this alone is enough to fill a socially anxious heart with dread. Job interviews also usually involve strangers and other unpredictable factors. All in all, a job interview is a leap into the unknown, and that's not pleasant for most people, socially anxious or not.

This is, however, one of those situations where you can try and pretend that your anxiety is just excitement. Indeed, there's plenty to be excited about anyway. You're taking proactive steps to improve your life by competing for a job, plus you have been called in for an interview based on the qualifications you have submitted in your CV. All of these are very positive things, and you have every reason to look at the whole thing in a very positive light. If you manage that shift in perspective, you might find that your fear and anxiety become much more manageable.

Furthermore, you have to consider the physical side that anxiety can sometimes have. There are substances in food and drink that can significantly increase your risk of getting anxious. Caffeine is a big-time perpetrator, especially when combined with sleep deprivation, so you should avoid both before an interview. As you may or may not know, energy drinks are loaded with caffeine, so don't make the mistake of thinking they are a better alternative to coffee. They will make you significantly more excited.

When it comes to food, you should certainly be well-fed so that your brain is working at its best, but you should avoid heavy meals. A healthy snack that's just enough to keep you going for a couple of hours at most should do great. You should also take some time after the meal to check if your teeth, clothes, and face are all clean. The last thing you want is this idea coming to you during the interview. All it takes is one glance at the corner of your mouth from the interviewer, and you might get overwhelmed, thinking you have something there. Destroy all possibilities beforehand.

Preparation is your friend as well. In the days leading up to the interview, you should learn as much about the company as humanly possible and come in armed to the teeth with information. Accumulate as much information as you can and use it to formulate answers that will resonate well with your potential employer. You can also use that information at home to try and come up with as many potential questions as you can. Consider what the company does and what they require of their employees and build on that. You will be able to predict a huge portion of their questions.

The next important thing is to get going on time. Interviews often happen in the morning, so make sure you get up early and give yourself plenty of time to prepare and get there. With or without SAD, getting there early is better than having to rush in or, God forbid, come in late.

Something that people with all sorts of anxieties often underestimate is the power of writing and journalizing. What I mean by that is that writing can have some powerful therapeutic effects on you, particularly if you are writing down the thoughts that are bothering you. If you've never done this, then you should certainly give it a try. You can even take a small pocket notebook with you and use it in the waiting room if your thoughts start getting the better of you.

The trick with writing stuff down is that it allows you to look at the contents of your mind more objectively. They are your thoughts, but you will be looking at them from what could be considered an outside perspective. When putting on paper, things tend to look more simplistic and sometimes even ridiculous. This will help you question some of the thoughts that are spinning around your head.

You should confront every one of your negative thoughts with logic and reason if you can. If you get to thinking that you aren't good enough for the job or that they won't like you, for instance, then you should consider the fact that you're already there. You were likely called up for the interview because your qualifications are satisfactory, now all you have to do is show the interviewers that you're the kind of person that can be worked with.

All in all, you should use the communication skills and the coping methods we have covered thus far while combining them with preparation and anxiety management before the interview itself. Remember always to push your thoughts as far away from yourself as you possibly can and focus on the aspects of the job and the interviewer, and don't even think about using alcohol to soothe the nerves before the interview. That would be a terrible idea.

Presentations and Public Speaking

In general, public speaking tends to be the number one nightmare scenario for most folks with social anxiety, and the same goes for many other kinds of public performance. Seeing as social anxiety is often all about the fear of embarrassment and judgment, it's only natural that public speaking will pose a significant problem. Even the most outgoing, extroverted individuals might get anxious before public speaking or presentations, depending on the context and gravity of the situation.

The first thing to do before public speaking is to make yourself as comfortable as you possibly can. Start by wearing an outfit that you are comfortable in but also very familiar with. It's a good idea to increase familiarity as much as you can to feel more secure. Leave as few things as you can to chance. If you have an outfit that you have been told looks good on you, then you should go with that one.

You must also remember what we said about fake self-confidence. Don't bother trying that route, because it is very likely to make things even worse. Instead, admit to yourself that you are nervous and come to terms with it for the time being. Remind yourself that it's natural to be nervous. If you know how to do it, it can be a good idea to let the audience know that you are nervous, but only if you can do it in a lighthearted manner that comes across as an ice-breaker above all.

Then again, that does depend on who exactly you are talking to. If you are holding a presentation in front of people you don't depend on; then you certainly have more leeway. It all boils down to how important this presentation is for your career as a whole. With some audiences, you can indeed outright ask for your nervousness to be excused, but it all depends on the context.

In general, a lot of the same rules will apply here as with job interviews, particularly when it comes to substances like caffeine. You should be as rested as you can and keep your head clear. Many teas can have soothing effects on you, such as chamomile. The truth is that since you struggle with social anxiety, you should replace coffee with tea altogether, not just before presentations.

If you are a long-term coffee drinker and your body is used to it, then abruptly skipping your coffee can cause problems of its own, such as headaches or irritability. Coffee isn't always a contributor to anxiety and that can vary from one person to another, but it has been shown that cutting caffeine out does help some people in the long run.

Another tip is not to try and make yourself sound like a master orator. Just because you are giving a speech doesn't mean that you have to speak a whole lot differently than you would in other contexts. In other words, don't try too hard. Keep the tone conversational and address your audience as if they were a regular conversational partner. This will make you sound more down to earth and will engage the audience and make them feel more comfortable.

If possible, get to know some members of the audience beforehand or, if that's not possible, get someone you know to come and sit among the crowd. As always, familiarity is an excellent ally in the struggle against anxiety.

You should also avoid talking about yourself except for that initial introduction if it's that kind of speech. Focus on the topic at hand and think about how you can bring it closer to your audience and keep it more straightforward. It's undoubtedly a good idea to try and put yourself in their shoes, as long as you're not doing it to look at and judge yourself from an outside perspective.

The only time you should think in that direction is when you can feel the onset of anxiety. Then, you can try to imagine yourself as a member of the audience, listening to someone giving a speech while showing some nervousness. Think about a time when you were listening to someone who seemed anxious. You probably didn't judge them or think they were inferior, stupid, or anything else of that nature. The truth is that most people are just like you in that regard, so don't worry about them thinking poorly of you.

Making presentations and giving speeches is a skill that can be exercised to artistry, so there are many other tips and tricks to make you better at it. For some people who are particularly gifted in this regard, the skill becomes the focal point of their career, as some jobs are all about public speaking. At any rate, if public speaking and presentations are something you're particularly interested in, it might be a good idea to check out my book on the subject, called "Never Deliver Another Crap Presentation Ever Again: 11 Most Effective Presentation Strategies." The book is available on Amazon Kindle.

Chapter Six: Further Tips on Surviving and Thriving in Workplace Situations

Apart from meetings, presentations, and job interviews, there are quite a few other work-related situations to deal with, of course. In this chapter, we'll take a look at three more big ones that tend to give socially anxious people extra trouble. Starting on a new job, interacting with your supervisors and bosses, and working with people who are just difficult by nature are all potentially stressful situations.

First Day at a New Job

Getting hired for a new job, especially if it's one that you've wanted, can be a somewhat strange situation when you have social anxiety. On the one hand, the fact that you got hired in the first place can be a confidence booster because it's a clear testament to your abilities and the fact that your employers liked you. The fact that you've nailed a job interview and managed to get hired will also show that you are undoubtedly capable of social interaction.

On the other hand, a new job is a major leap into the unknown. Even if you know all there is to know about your new job position; there can still be many people you will have to meet, many expectations you'll have to live up to, et cetera. These can all be powerful fuel for anxiety. Nonetheless, there are ways in which you can soften your landing and help yourself get acclimated to the new environment.

The first and simplest step is to look at the bright side and keep your thoughts focused on the positive side of what we just discussed. Based on the fact that you've made it to where you are, you should tell yourself that you are competent and capable of weathering through difficulties. After that, you should condition your mind to look for evidence supporting this claim. That way, you will remain focused on the positive side of things and contemplate each of your very real accomplishments instead of *potential* failures.

Of course, a good way to experience as little anxiety as possible is to be prepared. One of the most important things you can do is be well-rested for your first day. Any problems you might be having in your mind are always made worse by a lack of sleep, so make sure you get a good night's rest. It's also a good idea to try and create a peaceful and relaxing morning routine for when you wake up.

Have some breakfast and enjoy your morning cup of tea or coffee on the balcony if possible. Don't read the news and, if you can't help but think about the job, try to focus your thoughts on the accomplishment of getting hired. Overall, do whatever you find to be the most relaxing and make sure that you are as fresh as can be.

Making a positive first impression is undoubtedly desirable, but don't go out of your way obsessing over the idea. Most importantly, don't try to project any fake image in the office. You should be as authentic as possible and do your best to relax. Remember that you were interviewed and evaluated by experts whose job was to ensure that you are up to the task. Be content in that fact and just take the day as it comes.

You should also remind yourself whenever you must that a dose of anxiety about the first day at a new job is natural. Don't let yourself be frustrated or discouraged by the fact that you aren't 100% cold as ice – hardly anyone ever is.

Take advantage of your work itself. If your first day starts getting pretty busy, you should embrace the responsibilities and focus as much as you can on working. Distraction always plays well against anxiety attacks, social or otherwise. On top of that, depending on your workplace, you might get to meet a lot of new people. While this can certainly be a source of anxiety, it can also give you many useful distractions if you think about it the right way. Occupy your mind by absorbing all this new information and learning about your environment, and you will have less time to think anxious thoughts.

Another major source of anxieties of all kinds on the first day can arise if you set standards for yourself that are too high. Remember that you can't impress every single person you come into contact with and you might not be able to get every single thing done, so don't get carried away, taking on too many responsibilities as a means of impressing your bosses. Showing up on time, being genuine and pleasant, and getting some stuff done should be plenty to get you started off on the right foot. If you expect perfection from yourself, you are just setting yourself up for failure and a whole lot of stress.

Finally, something else that can help alleviate a lot of anxiety is the simple act of writing stuff down, both before and during the first day. If there is stuff to remember before you get to work, write it down. While at work, you should try and keep a notepad handy and write down whatever you can. Putting things on paper can take the weight off your mind and allow you to focus on other things while being confident that you won't forget anything.

All in all, you should be natural, avoid obsessive thinking whatever the subject might be, and stay focused on the work at hand. After the beginning, take it one day at a time and try to get acquainted with all of your colleagues as soon as possible. The sooner you get to know these people, the sooner the social aspect of your job will become second nature, and you'll start feeling at home.

Interacting with Your Manager

Keep in mind that you are not obligated to tell your employer about having SAD, not even if you have an actual diagnosis by a doctor. That means that you can avoid talking about it during the hiring process and for a while after starting a new job, but you can tell them later if you want.

In the US, you have this right because people with SAD are protected under the Americans with Disabilities Act. Furthermore, it might also be possible to acquire special accommodations at work if you disclose the conditions. That can go several ways, though, all depending on the kind of company you're working for and the type of job you're doing.

For one, if you hide your problem while getting hired and then come out of the blue asking for special treatment, your employer might think less of you for that, for obvious reasons. Secondly, as someone who is trying to beat their social anxiety, accommodation and special treatment are the last things you need, as we already explained. What then should you do?

Well, there's no reason why you couldn't tell your manager that you have SAD in a more-or-less informal manner. You don't have to put in any special requests or anything of the sort. Just tell your boss about the problem and explain that it's the reason why you might have certain difficulties at times. Tell them it's something you're working on and want to resolve.

The chances are good that your employer will be understanding or even helpful and supportive of your efforts to get better. If you have trouble fitting in, for instance, a good supervisor will help ease you in and assist you in becoming a part of the team. They can also help get your other coworkers to be supportive and understanding.

At that point, a kind and thoughtful employer might be the one actually to bring up the matter of accommodations. They might offer you a unique workspace, for instance, or help you minimize interaction in some other way. You should decline such offers and stay committed to getting along with people and practicing your social skills, as we discussed. Your job likely accounts for a huge chunk of your daily social interaction, so you want to make good use of it. If your employers started indulging your social anxiety, your problems could become worse than they have ever been before.

As far as interaction with supervisors goes, there's something else that concerns folks with social anxiety, and that's the fear that some people have of their boss. This is something that happens to people with or without social anxiety and usually goes back to a broader fear of authority in general. Sometimes, it's the fault of the authority figure if they are bad leaders who don't know how to communicate with their subordinates in a meaningful way and lead by positive example. However, unless your boss is your brother, sister, or childhood friend, your social anxiety is likely to make you fearful no matter how good of a leader they might be.

The first thing to do is to humanize your manager as much as possible. They aren't a robot who's there to keep an eye on you and dish out punishments for every infraction. It's entirely likely that your manager also has to worry about keeping their bosses happy and not messing up. This is a very common thing that most people have to deal with.

Furthermore, you should consider the facts and be aware of what the arrangement between you two actually entails. A supervisor's role is to ensure things are running smoothly, not to berate and fire people as soon as they make a mistake.

That might sound contradictory at first, but it's not when you think about it. Firing you or creating a major conflict would disrupt operations much, much more than giving you advice or calmly correcting you. You should always do your maximum, of course, but you don't have to be afraid of minor mistakes.

On top of that, a crucial part of any manager's job is to help the employees. He or she is there to address your concerns, get you on the right track, explain things to you, solve conflicts, and much more. Simply put, managers are people experts, not executioners. As such, you can perceive your manager as a coworker above all else, even if they have the power to fire you.

It's in the spirit of teamwork for everyone to feel like colleagues. As long as you are respectful and aware of your position in the company, you should be able to talk to your manager as you would to any other colleague. At the same time, heed all of their advice, value their opinion, be positive and eager about constructive criticism, and that should do it as far as interacting with your manager goes. Any fears will dissipate in time as well if you adopt this mindset.

Of course, staying focused on your work and keeping busy is the quintessential way to get over your fear of the boss. Now, this one is especially true if your supervisor is a bit tougher and not exactly the most pleasant person in your life. As long as you are focused on your job and doing the best you can, you should be good. On top of that, don't refrain from asking for help and advice. Many supervisors like it when employees do that, plus it will make you better at your job, so it's a win-win.

Working with Difficult People

A demanding, somewhat harsh boss is fairly low on the list of the worst people you can ever run into in your professional life, that's for sure. When you're struggling with social anxiety, difficult people can be tough to deal with, and they come in all forms, causing all sorts of problems.

Difficult people are those with whom communication is tough, even if you are the most sociable person in history. It's an umbrella term for people who are unstable, angry, humorless, overly critical, never satisfied, controlling, always confrontational, narcissistic, and much more.

As someone with SAD, you already know which of these tend to be the most problematic. When even constructive or mild criticism can hit you right in your anxiety, the people who go around with a mission to criticize everything and everyone can be a real nightmare. There are ways to deal with this, of course, or at least reduce the effect they have on you and make it more manageable.

The first thing to note is that it's okay to avoid these people. This is one of the exceptions to the anti-avoidance rule of battling social anxiety. Difficult people are avoided by *everyone,* not just socially anxious individuals, and it can be challenging to do so when you have to work in the same office.

One of the things you can try to do is talk to them to try and identify where the problem lies. People will rarely be difficult. After all, the office is not kindergarten, so it stands to reason that people have motives for acting a certain way or doing a certain thing. And if they direct negativity at you, then it might be a good idea to find out what that motive is.

Some people are difficult all the time and toward everybody, though. If you can see that they act like that with other people, then you can assume that the problem is not between the two of you. Such people usually have personal problems that they can't solve, which they then externalize in various negative, obnoxious ways. If you're unsure if you're the only target of this negativity, you can always ask other people if they've had similar experiences with the person you perceive as difficult.

In general, your best shields against difficult people is your self-control and your respectful conduct. Make sure that you are not difficult, exercise controlling your emotions as we discussed, and make double sure that you're treating people with respect by default, as long as they've never done anything to you. This immediately ensures that you won't have problems with 98% of people.

If you are as unlucky as to run into the 2% who will pick on people for no reason, and this is happening at the workplace, your first option is to try to reason with them and talk things out. Don't just try to placate them and do them favors, because this can make such people act even worse. Tell them you won't stand for their behavior and respectfully ask them to stop. The second option on the table is to ignore such people. Unfortunately, that often doesn't work out, and the person will continue being difficult.

Punching the person in the face might be very effective, but it's also a sure way to get fired, probably arrested, and maybe even sentenced, not to mention forced to pay damages. Overall it'll make your life fifteen times worse, so don't do it even if it's tempting. The real solution is to raise this issue with your superiors. This is perhaps the advantage of workplaces since they have a system for this type of thing.

However, keep in mind what this means. You will be going to the manager or someone even higher and telling them some very negative things about another employee. For one, this means that you must have a good explanation or, ideally, witnesses and evidence. Secondly, reporting them should be your last option on the table, never the first. It could result in disciplinary action, so you have to make sure that you've tried everything in your power to resolve the conflict.

In the vast majority of workplaces, being able to resolve conflicts and miscommunication is a skill that's expected of you. Unjustified reporting of colleagues to a higher authority can damage your reputation, not just with management but also with your coworkers.

Chapter Seven: Common Mistakes People with Social Anxiety Make

Before we get into the details of some other areas that you should work on to combat your social anxiety, we'll take a bit of time to rotate back to the more general side of things. In this chapter, I will walk you through a few of the most common mistakes that people with SAD tend to make, all of which can serve to perpetuate the condition or make it worse.

Obsessing over Mistakes

Socially anxious people tend to blow things out of proportion and make their social anxiety worse. With social anxiety, there is always a feeling of being constantly watched and evaluated by everyone around you. The tiniest of slip-ups can thus become something you spend an unhealthy amount of time thinking about. In severe cases, even the prospect of these tiny mistakes occurring in the near future can be a source of significant anxiety.

In reality, people are much more forgiving than you might think, and they are certainly less attentive to each and every one of your flaws than you believe. You can almost bet on that latter part. When you have social anxiety, it's easy to fall prey to the illusion that a few jumbled up words or a bit of a stumble as you walk, is harshly judged by everyone in the vicinity. In reality, people will usually either not pay attention or think nothing of it.

Remember that people have their own problems to worry about and they don't go around all day looking for things to laugh at in other people. So, instead of obsessing over that minor mistake you just made, you should try and put things in perspective. Did you stumble while walking up to begin your presentation? Will this tiny mistake matter after you've delivered a quality presentation? Will it matter a couple of days from now?

The truth is that everyone will forget all about it in a matter of hours or even minutes. Even if you receive a few chuckles, you shouldn't interpret those as ill-intentioned. After all, people make such small mistakes all the time, it's only natural, and it happens to everyone at some point.

Lack of Eye Contact

Eye contact is one of the most important aspects of interpersonal communication in humans and many other creatures as well. The eyes can tell a lot about how we are feeling, they can make what we're trying to say clearer, and sometimes they can replace words altogether.

Avoiding eye contact is something that socially anxious people will often do, however. The whole deal with eye contact can be viewed as something of a microcosm for social anxiety or at least a good part of it. For instance, because the eyes can give off so much information, maintaining eye contact can provide you with a distraction from your thoughts of anxiety because you will be processing that information and focusing on it.

When you break off eye contact, however, your mind will immediately shift to worrying about how that looks to the person you are interacting with. You will thus be focusing all of your attention on your every move instead of on the conversation, which perpetuates your social anxiety.

Breaking eye contact or never establishing it, to begin with is low-level avoidance. Maybe you didn't avoid the interaction with that person, but you are still avoiding aspects of social interaction that give you anxiety. As always, this bolsters your anxiety and allows it to grow stronger.

Think of eye contact as a smaller, condensed version of the entirety of social interaction, which you struggle with. Try to apply everything you have to do to improve your social communication in general. Above all, that means practice, so you need to exercise your ability to maintain eye contact every chance you get. The best way to get started is with people you are already comfortable with. You don't have to seek their help or organize anything. Instead, focus on eye contact and try to make it a subtle change in how you interact.

Overall, getting this right will be a great asset in your struggle to alleviate your social anxiety. Once you learn how to maintain proper eye contact, people will notice it, and they will respect you more. In the end, your confidence will receive a gradual boost as well.

Not Listening

While this is undoubtedly a mistake, it's often not something that people with SAD do intentionally. As such, the inability to listen to your conversational partner is one of the hallmarks of the disorder. If you think about it the right way, though, listening and being attentive can help you a lot in the way of subduing your anxiety. The key is not to think about yourself and or even the other person. Instead, focus on the substance of what is being said, contemplate the information, truly absorb it, and you will find that the person you are interacting with has your undivided attention. When you focus, things like eye contact will also come naturally.

It's all about being an active listener instead of a passive one who wants to get through the conversation as quickly as possible and get the hell out of there. To truly and actively listen to a person, you need to look for small cues and clues that they give in their speech and body language. These subtleties are the stuff you can use to develop a conversation further.

The best way to do that is to ask questions based on the signs you detect because questions are very good at keeping conversations going. Avoid just agreeing, disagreeing, or nodding. Look into the subtext of what a person is saying and the reasons or motives behind the things they're saying. If you focus enough, you will find it's straightforward to construct simple inquiries that can keep the talk going, and when you sprinkle some of your opinions in there, you will have yourself an actual, two-way conversation. Before you know it, you will be lost in the conversation and will forget about yourself, which is the key to keeping your social anxiety at bay.

Trouble with Names

An inability to remember someone's name after you've just met them is a common problem for folks with social anxiety, but it happens to healthy people too. Like many of the other issues we discussed, this one too tends to perpetuate your social anxiety and make you feel even worse. To an already anxious mind, the prospect of having to ask for someone's name twice or sometimes even thrice is very unsettling for fear of coming across as stupid or overly nervous, which always makes matters worse.

This is a problem you can work on, however, and in many cases, mending this issue tends to alleviate social anxiety. The problem itself has much more to do with your short-term memory than with social anxiety, so it'll take some mental exercise to solve it. The two main tricks to use are association and repetition.

When it comes to an association, it's all about making a quick mental note of some unique characteristic that the stranger possesses and associating that characteristic with their name. Do they have pink hair, strange teeth, a certain distinct voice, or something else that you notice straight away? Keep in mind that having no distinctive characteristics is, in itself, a characteristic. You can use all of this stuff by just making that connection the moment you meet the person, and it's going to be pretty difficult to forget "Joe with the weird tooth," for instance.

On top of association, you should see if you can repeat the person's name multiple times as soon as possible, preferably aloud, of course. Use their name right away in the sentences and questions that you put into the initial exchange, and also repeat the name internally a few times. Practice these two tricks, and you are bound to see an improvement soon. Association can help you strengthen your short-term memory in other contexts as well, not just socializing.

Obsessing over the Anxiety Itself

While it might sound like a bit of a cliché, the truth is that the more you think and worry about your anxiety, the worse it can get. Certainly, you have to make efforts toward beating this problem, but that doesn't entail thinking dreadful thoughts about your anxiety all the time, obsessing over how difficult it is, how there's something broken in your head, et cetera. These thoughts serve no purpose other than to reinforce the issue and keep you in the doldrums.

Don't let this illness define you and become the central theme of your identity. While using strategies and techniques to combat your social anxiety, you should focus on your strengths and good qualities. Your social anxiety is just some extra baggage that you're trying to get rid of, not your core characteristic. Your SAD is what prevents your true characteristics from coming out and being projected onto the world through your social interactions. In other words, it keeps the real you hidden and suppressed.

Most importantly, don't spend hours on end dwelling on things after an unsuccessful interaction. If you do mess up in some way, you should do your best to forget the whole thing after the fact. You can do this by running errands, taking care of some chore, or focusing on your work. The worst thing you could do is lock yourself in a dark room and dive into the negativity.

Treating Yourself Badly

If you want to feel better and more at ease, you should make sure that you practice what you preach in the sense that you are treating yourself well. This goes beyond just being too hard on yourself and indulging in self-criticism. To treat yourself well, you should strive to live a healthy lifestyle, give yourself rewards and incentives, and taking time off when you need to.

When we don't like ourselves, we tend to convince ourselves that there's nothing in us that's worth liking. If you think like this, it stands to reason that you will always assume that other people only see the worst in you too. As you know, this is one of the driving forces behind social anxiety. It doesn't work for everyone, but you might be surprised how much a training regimen can benefit your overall mental health on top of improving your physical shape.

Improving your overall health is one of the best things you can do for yourself, but it tends to be a bit subtle as far as rewards go. It's not a bad idea to do something nice for yourself, such as get a dog, for instance. A dog will require regular walks and all sorts of other activities, which will keep you on the move and your mind focused on positive things.

Surrendering to Negativity

If you try hard enough, almost anything in life can be flipped on its head and perceived from some positive perspective. You mustn't surrender yourself completely to negative and hopeless thinking. Focus on your path toward beating your anxiety and keep your mind on each and every success you have experienced. As for failures, unless they have provided you with clear and valuable lessons, forget all about them.

Furthermore, even anxiety can be a positive thing sometimes. Remember what we said about anxiety being natural. The problem only arises when you lose control, as anxiety itself certainly serves its purpose in healthy people. That's not to say that you should go around thinking about how sick you are all the time. You should keep in mind that anxiety can sometimes be helpful as well because it can help us avoid dangerous situations.

Of course, caring about how you are perceived and about the impression you make, especially in your professional life, is perfectly normal and good. Remember, the objective of your struggle is not to stop caring about what people think altogether. The aim is to stop obsessing over it and letting it keep you down. Furthermore, socially anxious folks might sometimes interpret things like constructive criticism or friendly advice as personal attacks or insults when they aren't. You need to be mindful of the subtleties of what people are saying and understand that not everyone is out to get you, even if they are critical.

Hiding and Shame

Your social anxiety disorder isn't something you chose, and it's not a result of some mistakes you consciously made – it is an illness. You might have social anxiety because of the way you were treated in your childhood or simply as a result of genetics, but it's virtually impossible at any rate for this to be your fault, so there's nothing to be ashamed of.

You don't have to hide the fact that you have social anxiety. You can benefit immensely from letting people know about your problem, especially if they are your loved ones, other trusted people, or your superiors at work. I'm not talking just about the advice that you can receive. As counterintuitive as it might sound, the truth is that revealing your social anxiety to others can be very liberating and ease a lot of the tension when you're interacting with them. Not to mention, people in professional environments, especially managers, will usually be understanding and thoughtful when informed about this problem.

Finally, of course, it goes without saying that you shouldn't go through this problem alone if you don't have to. Non-experts might not be the most helpful when it comes to advice, no matter how well-intentioned and close to you they are, but just talking about your problem can make you feel much better.

Giving Your Anxiety Room to Grow

An idle mind is the devil's playground, especially when you have any anxiety or depression. Distractions are your greatest allies both in individual situations and in general. Whenever you can, you should strive to keep yourself busy with anything you can. You can read, do work-related activities, engage in some creative endeavor, or just exercise. As long as you're not pushing yourself too far, it will do you good, whatever it is.

Getting a new hobby or two is an excellent idea if you have time to fill up. Certain hobbies can be very healthy for you both physically and mentally, leading you on a path toward self-improvement. A mix of not thinking about your anxiety and working to improve yourself in some regard is one of the best ways to fight anxiety disorders, confidence issues, and a range of other problems. Just be productive and keep your mind occupied – it is a strategy that has worked for about as long as humanity has been around.

As unbelievable as it is, socially anxious folks will often go straight into isolation mode after experiencing an unpleasant situation. They will shut themselves in and dwell on their problems for days, not understanding that they are directly feeding their anxiety and making sure it gets even worse next time. This is the exact time when you need to stay busy the most. Get out and get some stuff done and don't let your mind wander.

Avoidance

It really can't be overstated how much of a problem avoidance is when you have a social anxiety disorder. If your disorder had to eat, avoidance would be considered its favorite food. Social anxiety disorder is an illness that you must never accommodate in any way or adapt yourself and your lifestyle to your anxiety's whim. After all, keeping you closed off and isolated from the world, alone with your troubled mind, is precisely what your illness wants to do.

Of course, it's entirely true that some folks might enjoy taking some time to recharge after prolonged social interaction, and sometimes we all feel like staying in with a cup of tea and a book

– these things are natural. However, you should always ask yourself why you're really refusing to go out or are continually putting off running an errand that requires social interaction, and try to be as honest with yourself as possible.

Are you exhausted, or are you avoiding contact because you are afraid of interaction? Sometimes, it's a good idea to go out even if you are tired, just as a form of exercise. Overall, you should seek out those social situations that frighten you and tackle your fears head-on.

Chapter Eight: Assertiveness Tips

Your level of assertiveness is, of course, closely related to your social skills and also your level of self-confidence. For people with social anxiety, difficulties with asserting one's self seem to be a universal problem. Being assertive is sometimes viewed as the opposite of social anxiety, and this is for good reason. Whereas the socially anxious try their best to stay on the sidelines and hide from all spotlights, assertive individuals have no problem getting right in there and standing right in the middle of the light. Some folks not only do this out of necessity but they also actually enjoy it because they like the attention.

There are also quite a few misconceptions out there concerning assertiveness and what it means for your interaction with the world and the way you come across. For example, people sometimes conflate assertiveness with egocentrism. It's not about always getting what you want or just attracting attention for attention's sake. Assertive people know when and how to present their opinions and how to negotiate compromises while taking everyone's interests into account. Asserting yourself and being imposing and obnoxious are two very different things. In general, it's not about the selfish pursuit of your interests – it's just confidence and social skill.

Assertiveness is about being proactive, involved, and agreeable as long as your interests aren't being shamelessly violated. This is where assertive folks will apply the long-forgotten art of saying no to people. Assertive people understand that the path toward popularity is not through passivity and constant submission, which is another characteristic that helps assertive people rise through the ranks of their respective organizations quicker. Giving into everything people ask of you and just constantly agreeing and nodding your head at everything is a bad way to go through life, let alone a business environment.

Being assertive also means that you are confident enough in your opinions that you can always be honest and say what you mean, even if it leads to disagreement. There is nothing fundamentally wrong with disagreement in any way. It isn't impolite or unfriendly by default, and it certainly isn't something to fear when rational adults are having a conversation.

Saying "no" is a concept that goes far beyond just that, though. It's also about setting boundaries and making sure that you are respected instead of used, for example. This is a very important aspect of assertiveness, but it's also one of the most difficult for socially anxious folks.

Try to think of a hypothetical scenario where your boss politely asks you to come in on Sunday if you can. Of course, you don't want to do anything of the sort, but at the same time, you want to impress your superiors with hard work, especially if you're new. But then again, if you accept now, you might become that one person who is always called in.

In such a situation, you get to be both smart and assertive. You say yes to your boss's request that one time, but when he asks you to do the same thing again next week, you draw the line and say you can't come in. That is assertiveness in a nutshell. You would have established yourself as the person who can go the extra mile when you feel like it but can also say no and look out for your interests.

As you can see, assertiveness is something that could prove very difficult with social anxiety. Like the other things we discussed thus far, however, assertiveness too can be practiced, in turn helping you in your fight against social anxiety. This whole explanation of what assertiveness is has already given you a few tips on how to behave assertively, but we will take a look at some more techniques and advice that could help you get to that point.

Becoming More Assertive

Now you know what it means to be an assertive person, but how do you go about becoming like that yourself? Well, as you can imagine, it has a lot to do with confidence and social skills. As such, assertiveness can perhaps be viewed as a testament that you have reached an advanced stage in your transformation from social anxiety to healthy sociability. As we mentioned earlier, an assertive individual is more or less the opposite of a reserved and anxious one.

Your first step is to prepare yourself for discomfort. Even if you have improved your social skills, learned how to maintain a conversation, and gathered a healthy bit of self-confidence, truly asserting yourself can still be challenging. This is because you will be moving away from mere back-and-forth communication and entering the realm of exerting influence on others. Another reason why it's difficult is that you will now be revealing a bit more of your inner self, and that can be tough.

Keep in mind that while assertiveness means you are looking out for your interests and needs, getting what you want isn't the essence. The essence is meaningful communication between human beings on a higher level. Having your needs met is just a positive result and benefit that you sometimes reap when you know how to ask, but the emphasis is on the word *ask*. Stepping over others, manipulating them, working behind their backs, sabotaging them, or doing anything else that's immoral in the interest of pursuing your self-interest is not assertiveness.

To be assertive, you should always operate from a position of respect or, more precisely, mutual respect. Something else to consider is that being assertive isn't just about expressing your needs and opinions for the sake of trying to get some benefit. It's somewhat two-sided actually in that you are making things easier for the other party as well by being assertive and clear. It will be easier for them to react and, most importantly, it will be easier to reach compromises and ensure everyone is satisfied.

If you are completely new to the concept, you can start very, very basic and straightforward, practicing on your own. Start by learning the three-part assertive sentence structure. The first part of the sentence is the word "I," with which most assertive sentences begin. The second part is your feeling that you are expressing in the form of a verb such as "like" or "hate." The third part is the descriptive bit that explains what you are trying to say.

And so, a very simple example of a highly assertive sentence would be along the lines of: "I hate when you look at your phone when I speak." If you have been passive and withdrawn for a long time, you might be surprised by how rarely you have uttered such simple sentences. Pay attention in the future and you'll see, then make it your objective to use as many such sentences as you can when talking to people.

You'll have to practice it for a while before it becomes second nature, but once it does, it will work perfectly with the ability as mentioned earlier to say "no" to people. Your position will be much more firm in the future, and you will become more formidable. Keeping your speech clear, simple, and to the point will help you exert more control and have an easier time getting used to assertiveness.

Of course, you should also make sure that you don't overdo it. Keep your expressions relevant to the context and the conversation's topic. Don't just go around all day looking for excuses to say that you don't like this or that or trying to boss people around. Opinions can undoubtedly be unwelcome when unsolicited, although they can be justified by the nature of some conversations, in which case you don't have to wait for people to ask what you think.

If someone is discussing a specific topic with you, such as politics, it stands to reason that they are already interested in your opinions so that you can speak your mind. What you don't want to do, of course, is go up to people and throw your views and beliefs at them for no reason.

Additional Tips

Remember what we talked about earlier when we were discussing conversation skills and interaction. A lot of that stuff will come into your efforts to become more assertive because, as you can see, communication is one of the main ways in which we assert ourselves. Assertiveness means that you are neither passive nor aggressive but are somewhere in the middle.

Your passive ways are something you have to leave behind if you are to become more assertive and accomplished in your communication with others. Your passive style of communication has probably served you well as a means of avoiding all confrontation and other unexpected situations that you can't control, but how much good has it done you? All it has done is make you miss opportunities, internalize and bottle up negativity, and torture your mind in isolation.

Apart from verbal communication, there are behaviors and other things that are marks of an assertive person. Consider what we said about body language, but make sure that you are focused as well. Assertive people are very present and grounded in the moment and place they are in. They pay attention to everything around them and react accordingly.

How you speak is also important. You should speak clearly, distinctly, and with the proper tone. Don't yell at people, obviously, but apply enough force in your voice to be heard whenever you speak. Your voice should be strong and reliable, but also relaxed. Relaxed also means even and smooth when it comes to voices because you don't want the color, tone, and volume of your voice to be all over the place, changing erratically. That would send a clear message that you struggle to control your conduct.

Honesty is a virtue that goes a long way toward when you're trying to be assertive. These two things work so well together that some people outright consider them to be synonymous. When you are speaking honestly and from the heart, you will expend no energy on making the things you say seem legitimate because you know they are.

Indeed, lying is hard work for most people, and it always carries a dose of anxiety with it. Because of all this, you might not be able to speak as confidently, clearly, and naturally when you're lying. Only a small number of people can do this, but being good at lying is nothing to be proud of anyway, so you shouldn't concern yourself with that.

All in all, even in order to become assertive, you have to assert. It's only after you decide to change your approach to life and people and take the first step that you will be able to become assertive. The best part is that by trying to become more assertive, you will be practicing both your social skills and working on your confidence.

As you can see, it's all connected and all of these aspects of how you interact with the world feed into each other. If you're a confident person, it's not too difficult to assert yourself. If you assert yourself, your confidence will receive a boost, especially if you assert yourself successfully. Once you try to get out there, you will feel it all on your skin, and you will have a much better idea of where you are exactly and how much work you'll have to put into yourself.

Benefits of Assertiveness

You have undoubtedly noted quite a few benefits of assertiveness by this point, but we'll take a look at some other ways in which being more assertive can change aspects of your life for the better. With your parents, spouse, children, siblings, friends, or strangers – assertiveness has benefits in all aspects of life that entail any interpersonal communication, far beyond just your workplace.

Take relationships, for example. Most problems people have in this regard usually go back to miscommunication and an inability to properly externalize our needs. When people can't express their needs to their partners, it's no surprise when those needs aren't met.

Since assertiveness is all about making your needs known, it benefits relationships immensely. An assertive personality and a well-developed set of communication skills are a combination that makes people fare much better in relationships and marriage.

A lack of assertiveness also contributes to fights and arguments, in all sorts of relationships, not just romantic. If you go on suppressing your opinions and needs for long enough, letting them all bottle down and fester deep inside, you are likely going to snap at some point. Some of the worst arguments in your life can occur exactly like this.

The reason why being more assertive reduces social anxiety is that it shows you how being open and expressive toward people is a good thing. This is how you fight your fear of opening up and exposing yourself you people, which is one of the central fears in social anxiety. Once you see how people tend to agree with you or at least try to make a compromise, it can be quite a revelation. You'll also find that getting what you want is often not difficult at all.

Assertiveness can soothe anxiety and stress in general, though, not just in social situations. The more you assert your point of view and express yourself, the fewer things you'll have suppressed inside, burdening your mind. You have probably noticed how those people who appear to be the most care-free are usually those who are outgoing, expressive and have no problem saying what's on their mind. This is all because they are channeling their thoughts and feelings outward in a healthy manner.

Asking for your interests to be considered and your needs to be met are all forms of self-care and self-love. This is how self-confidence and self-esteem are nurtured and strengthened. Just as we talked about earlier, there can be no high confidence without loving and respecting yourself, and what better way is there to do this than to make sure you are given what you deserve. As long as you remember that you should be active and expressive, not aggressive, you will also get more respect from others by being assertive.

Perhaps the greatest benefit that comes with time is the feeling of being back in control. As you well know, one of the worst things about social anxiety is how it deprives you of control and makes you feel helpless. When you are assertive, you will feel like you are in charge of your life. Just as importantly, you will also influence the world around you, getting people to change their minds, to look at you differently, et cetera. When you are passive and reserved, you are inconsequential, but when you assert yourself, you exert influence.

Assertiveness will make you an overall more fulfilled and stable individual. You will gain respect both from others and from yourself. All of this is why assertiveness is one of the greatest achievements of this anti-anxiety struggle and a true sign that you have been transformed. Just remember not to get ahead of yourself and always maintain the balance between advocating for your needs and taking into account the needs of others.

Chapter Nine: How to Make Friends, Nurture Friendships at Work and Home

Whether it's about performing better at home, at parties, or at work, the questions of social anxiety usually revolve around one crucial aspect of the human condition, and that's friendship. This is where it all begins and sometimes ends. Making friends, keeping friends, deepening your relationship with a friend – all of these are matters that most socially anxious people have to struggle with.

Some who suffer from this dreaded condition are lucky enough to have a couple of close friends in their lives, usually childhood friends, who are there to provide support. Friends can help get you out there, pick you up when you stumble, help you establish new contacts, and practice your social skills. Some friends are more understanding or more equipped to give valuable advice than others, but no matter how much concrete assistance they are giving directly, their existence in itself can be a major relief.

Indeed, the importance and value of friends in our lives can't be overstated. A friend isn't just someone you go out with for a cup of coffee or dinner. True friendship is about much more than having a few laughs on the weekend and having fun in general. All of these things are certainly a part of it, but ultimately, friendship is about partaking in someone else's life while they also partake in yours. That includes good and bad moments alike; joy and pain, better and worse.

Socially anxious folks who already have a close friend or two are at a solid advantage right from the start, and this can make all the difference. That's why social anxiety counseling sometimes focuses solely on teaching the patient to establish and maintain friendships. While friendship is something that socially anxious folks dream about but don't have because of their anxiety, there is a positive flip side to that situation. Namely, slowly learning how to make friends and embarking upon the journey of meeting one is, in and of itself, an exercise in subduing your social anxiety while being the objective at the same time.

As we discussed early on in this book, human beings are social creatures by nature. Certainly, there have probably been plenty of people who made it through life without friends, but the benefits of friendship have been measured to a certainty. Apart from just providing moral support, having friends has its health benefits as well. Indeed, people who have meaningful friendships in their lives tend to live longer and experience fewer health problems in general.

Many of the things we have discussed thus far should make it easier for you to establish contact with new people. Confidence, assertiveness, and communication will often play the most important roles in your establishment of new relationships, whether they are in romance, business, or friendship. However, there is still quite a bit to learn, and the art of making and keeping friends entails many of its own tips and techniques.

We will cover such information in this chapter, and you will get a better idea of how the things you've learned earlier come together and apply to meeting new people. If you truly have no friends in your life, however, success might require some drastic changes in your life and especially your way of thinking. Loneliness can sometimes provide its own sort of harmful comfort to us, keeping us inert and disinterested.

If we spend too much time being alone, we can forget all about the finer things that life has to offer. Before starting to make friends, you will have to start seeing your life in a new light, and a good way to start is to make things like loneliness more bearable.

Dealing with Isolation and Loneliness

The most immediate thing to do in this regard is to alleviate some of the weight that loneliness and isolation might be exerting on your mind. Learning how to deal with loneliness might sound counterintuitive at first when all you want to do is make friends, but it's certainly a useful skill. Besides, you want to do what you can to start feeling better right away since making friends might turn out to be a process that takes some time.

Having an easier time while being lonely mostly revolves around matters of perspective and state of mind. It's one of those things that depend mostly on what you do in your head.

First and foremost, "dealing with loneliness and isolation" doesn't mean reconciling with this as your eternal reality or fate. It doesn't mean accepting loneliness as normal and not doing anything to fix it. What you do want to do, however, is make this just a little easier on yourself while you're working on the long-term solutions.

What you want to do is ask yourself what could constitute a quality alternative to socializing and spending time with friends. For the vast majority of people, that alternative is productivity. If you are lonely and have no friends, the worst thing to do is sit at home all the time and taking cheap, instant gratification from things like TV shows. You need to engage in things that pertain to your life, not the lives of fictional TV characters.

Of course, one of the best ways to do this is to pick up a valuable hobby. A hobby is a somewhat misunderstood concept among some folks who think that it has to consist of nothing but leisure, but a hobby can be a very productive endeavor. You can take up cardio exercise outdoors, enroll in a gym program, take up an art such as drawing or writing, read classic literature, or start learning a new language. The options are virtually limitless.

There are two questions you can ask to help you determine if a certain hobby is right for you. Firstly, is it going to make you feel fulfilled and lead to self-improvement? Secondly, does it provide opportunities to establish new contacts and make friends? Generally speaking, the first question is more important, but seeing as you are fighting social anxiety, the second one is perhaps just as important if you want to boost your chances of meeting someone.

An important aspect of dealing with loneliness is learning to deal with rejection. Rejection is something that happens even to the most sociable people you can imagine. It probably happens to them more than to the average persons because they initiate so much communication with people, so they increase their statistical chances of getting rejected.

It is a plain and simple fact that rejection means absolutely nothing in the long run. People can have so many reasons to reject you in a million different contexts and ways that there is just no use trying to come up with some general "rule" as to why you have been rejected. Don't think in that direction at all because it will only bring you down. Don't even try to explain it. What you need to do is master the art of moving on and not giving a damn.

The best way to move on after getting rejected is to focus on the fact that you have lost absolutely nothing. This is the same thing that people use to motivate themselves to initiate contact, and it works just fine after the fact as well. Think about it: Yesterday, you didn't know this stranger existed, and you lived just fine. After this rejection, you go back to living your life without this stranger playing any part in it. You can see how nothing has changed whatsoever, and you'll probably never see that person again either way, so there is no reason to dwell on it.

That's essentially all there is to dealing with loneliness. You make sure you're doing something with your life and working toward improving yourself, and you get ready to deal with rejection. You will feel thus feel much better as you continue working on your social anxiety and waiting for that special contact.

Making Friends

Throughout this book, you have learned plenty about how to establish contact with people, even strangers, and how to get conversations going and continuing for a while. All of that stuff is generally the first step toward making friends. As simplistic as it sounds, you have to get out there and talk to people, that's it. There's no way for a friend to fall from the sky while you're in your house all afternoon watching TV shows.

If you still go to the grocery store, then you have some semblance of a chance of meeting somebody, yes, but those chances are practically non-existent. If you go to work via public transportation, your chances are further increased, but if you use a car, you're just shipping yourself from home to work in a box.

The one way you might be able to make a friend from home is over the Internet, but that's at least some kind of proactive approach, so it doesn't exactly qualify as "waiting for a friend to fall from the sky." When you establish contact, you will eventually have to go out and meet that person as well, so it's better than doing nothing.

However, the one true way of making friends is to fill up your free time with meaningful, outdoor activities. You have to take part in life instead of letting it go on outside of your door. Take up a hobby that facilitates that as we discussed, but also try to seek out social situations whenever possible actively. For instance, instead of ordering a pizza, go outside and get some food yourself. Adopt this principle throughout your life and always go for the more social option when you have a choice.

Furthermore, as you work toward subduing your social anxiety in the office, try to talk more and more with your coworkers, especially those that are of similar age and have interests that at least remotely resemble yours. If you click with someone, there will be an opportunity to go out with them sooner or later. Coworkers often go out for a drink or dinner after work, so you are bound to get invited if you start socializing more. These evenings will be great opportunities to meet other people as well and expand your network further.

This one is a bit of a no-brainer, but do your best to embrace every invitation and opportunity to attend a social event. Don't overlook family ones either because those can be very beneficial for practicing your social skills. Family gatherings might even be among the best such opportunities because there tends to be a lot of questioning, catching up, updating, criticism, and other stuff that triggers social anxiety. As such, family gatherings are great for you to test your progress or toughen up.

In essence, the process of making friends, or at least the process of trying to make friends, is as simple as can be. All you have to do is practice your social skills and always take steps to maximize your chances of ending up in social situations. If you do these two things, meeting new people is unavoidable.

The somewhat difficult part comes after you make the acquaintance. This is because you will have to read people, talk to them about a range of different subjects, see them in varying environments, et cetera. Don't worry too much about it, though, because when you meet someone compatible with you, whether as a friend or a romantic partner, it will be fairly obvious to you. You may have forgotten or may have never known in the first place because of your anxiety, but compatible people do "click."

Nurturing Friendships in the Long Term

Meeting someone new and clicking with them is one thing, but maintaining the contact, building the relationship, and then nurturing it for years to come is something else entirely. In part, this tends to come naturally once you establish a meaningful connection with someone, but it can certainly be a struggle, especially if you've never had the opportunity to learn how to do it.

One of the key things to understand when it comes to friendship is that quality trumps quantity ten times out of ten. Having fifty "friends" and not establishing a deep connection with them is almost entirely a waste of time. Unless you're a salesperson or a promoter of some kind, and your livelihood depends on networking, there is no reason to have that many friends. The truth is that you need two or three actual friends at most. Other people are just acquaintances and, of course, family members and relatives.

You probably understand this already as someone with social anxiety, but your social media friends and followers are worthless in the way of filling the void. It's great having two or three friends, but just one is worth much more than social media, that's for sure.

To maintain long-term friendships, you have to understand a friend's value, but you must also understand what a friend is. Your friend is a person you can spend time with, without any filter or mask. They know exactly who you are, what you are like, and they choose to spend their valuable time with you not *despite,* but *because* of what you are like. When people associate with you despite something, they usually do it because they are trying to get something out of you. Of course, in friendship, all of this goes both ways.

Furthermore, a friend is the one person you can turn to at any time when the going gets tough. They are the person you can call out for a cup of coffee just because you feel like you have to talk about a certain thing. They are the person who will drop by your place when you need company.

Most friendships are rarely truly tested in life, but you do need to be ready for all sorts of turmoil, just in case. Don't take your friendship for granted. You should understand that life can complicate things no matter how well you get along with your friends.

It stands to reason that you also have to value your friend and the special bond between you. This appreciation is demonstrated organically, through action, not with words or gifts. The best way to show your friend that you appreciate them is to be honest with them all the time and be there for when they need you too. Also, when you have a problem with a friend, you need to bring it up and talk it all out. Even if it leads to an argument or a fight, your friendship will be even stronger once the dust has settled.

Last but not least, you and your friend must not be toxic influences in each other's lives. A friend's support is perhaps best demonstrated when you compete for the same goal. If you succeed where your friend has failed, a true friend will be happy for you regardless because even when you are competing, he is above all your friend.

Accept your friend's flaws, don't expect perfection, and make sure that you are always available to them. Make sure that you know what their long-term hopes and ambitions are and support them on their journey. Don't ever jeopardize your friendship for any personal gain and stay loyal. But most importantly, make sure that everything flows both ways.

Chapter Ten: Panic Attack Tips and Strategies

Panic attacks are something that people often refer to when discussing matters related to social and other types of anxiety. Anxiety attacks and panic attacks are not the same things, but if you are experiencing episodes of fear and dread, it will be useful to acquaint yourself with panic attacks as well.

Anxiety attacks tend to come on gradually and are usually connected to a certain phobia such as, in your case, social. Panic attacks, on the other hand, are very sudden, and their cause or trigger might not always be readily apparent. Something else that's worth mentioning is that anxiety attacks are still a fairly loosely defined concept because they aren't listed in the American Psychiatric Association's Diagnostic and Statistical Manual of Mental Disorders.

As you might imagine, unexpected panic attacks are those that strike suddenly and without warning or apparent reason. Expected panic attacks occur after being triggered by an external influence, which usually comes from a phobia you have. The main difference here is that expected panic attacks can be sourced, but they too can be "unexpected" if a certain trigger shows up out of nowhere and sets you off, of course.

Panic attacks are something that can occur naturally in healthy individuals on rare occasions if they experience any psychological overload. If panic attacks occur regularly, however, this might be indicative of a panic disorder. Furthermore, panic attacks tend to last for a shorter period of around ten minutes or so, while symptoms of anxiety can go on and on for much longer than that. Panic attacks and disorders can be an extension of various anxiety disorders, but they also can be a source of new anxiety.

Symptoms and Causes of Panic Attacks

For instance, a panic attack can sometimes occur as a sort of culmination of a prolonged period of anxiety. If you are anticipating a problematic situation such as a job interview or a presentation, your anxiety might lead you on a path of worrying and dread as the event draws near. And then, when it happens, you might be overcome by a paralyzing, sudden fear that takes things to a whole new level. This is how panic attacks happen for many people who struggle with anxiety.

Many of the symptoms can be similar to those of anxiety, albeit usually more intense. They are generally categorized into emotional and physical symptoms. On the emotional plain, the big one that's shared between anxiety and panic is fear, of course. Panic attacks, however, can entail a fear of death as well as your heart begins to pump harder and harder.

Panic attacks can sometimes feel like an onset of a heart attack to those who have no experience with the latter, which is terrifying. This state can also lead to feelings of being "beside" one's self. In other words, a panic attack can dislodge you from reality and even from your own mind for a minute or two. Physical symptoms are virtually all shared between anxiety and panic attacks, although they can be significantly worse during an outbreak of panic.

Essentially, one of the best ways to identify a panic attack is by the fact that it is a highly disruptive outburst. Unless it's severe, anxiety is something that you can operate under and soldier through, but panic attacks will usually outright impair you. Since your brain will go into full fight-or-flight mode during a panic attack, your body will be all but autonomous.

The truly scary thing is that this can happen at the worst possible times, such as when you're driving. This is why panic disorders are usually a more severe type of condition than anxiety disorders. As such, panic attacks can hardly kill you directly, but they can impair you to the point where serious harm can occur.

Unexpected panic attacks can be rooted very deeply, sometimes in events that have occurred years ago or during childhood and have since been suppressed deep inside. Indeed, just like anxiety, panic disorders can be connected to past trauma. A wide range of psychological problems like phobias, depression, or substance abuse can also be the culprits. Panic attacks can also be caused by physical illnesses, especially chronic ones like heart problems, asthma, diabetes, et cetera.

Keep in mind that panic attacks, as well as general anxiety, can be provoked by various substances as well, some of which might be completely normal for your daily life. Caffeine is known to contribute to anxiety in some cases, but it could also be some medication you might be taking. If you are indeed on medication, it's a good idea to consult with your doctor and see if it could be a contributing factor to panic attacks. Withdrawal from drugs but also alcohol and nicotine can also go a long way toward giving you a panic attack.

Also, like anxiety disorders, panic disorders can arise from a genetic predisposition. If you have a family history of such problems, then it's certainly something to look out for. Attacks are just incidents, but when they are recurring, that is indicative of a panic disorder.

A distinct characteristic of panic disorders is that they also involve obsessive worrying and fear of future attacks. Attacks can be so bad sometimes that they all but traumatize you, staying in memory for quite a while. This is why even being reminded of something that had triggered panic attacks in the past can trigger new ones. It's a self-perpetuating cycle of fear and dread. It is essentially a fear of fear itself.

All in all, if you can't think straight and if you feel like your limbs are giving out and your heart is pounding in your ears and you're about to lose all control, it's probably some degree of a panic attack. If you are convinced that you are about to pass out, experience a heart attack, or collapse, those are all good indications that you're having a panic attack. Panic attacks can make your chest tense up and give you pain too. It's things like this that give panic attacks a whole new level of scary as they can truly convince you that you're dying, especially if you 've never experienced them before.

The line can get a bit blurred sometimes, though, so it's not always clear what's at play. When someone suffers from social anxiety at a more severe level, certain panic attacks can feel as though they are just more of the same, only a tad stronger this time.

Dealing with Panic Attacks in the Moment

These attacks can be truly terrifying, and while some degree of anxiety can be managed, panic attacks difficult to control. Worse yet, they can manifest in ways that make your troubles very obvious to everyone present, which can perpetuate the fear and make things even worse. Nonetheless, there are quite a few things that you can do to keep these outbursts at bay.

A common way in which people deal with panic attacks and stressful situations, in general, is through breathing exercises, particularly deep breathing. Since panic attacks tend to cause that constricting feeling in your chest, you will likely breathe way too fast and shallow or not enough at all. Either way, you will not be getting enough oxygen, which greatly exacerbates feelings of anxiety and panic. Next time you get an attack, try to inhale for four seconds, hold air in your lungs for four seconds, and then exhale for four seconds.

You should keep the 4-4-4 approach going for a while until you feel that you're starting to calm down. It's a simple exercise, but it happens to work wonders for some people. The important thing is to get fresh oxygen into your system at a sufficient but controlled, gradual rate. A steady stream of oxygen tends to alleviate many physical symptoms such as dizziness, tremors, heightened heart rate, and other issues. To ensure that you are getting the most out of each breath, make sure that your breathing is diaphragmatic, meaning that your stomach is expanding when you breathe in.

Furthermore, experience affords you familiarity, even in things as upsetting as these panic attacks. If you've been through them before, you should do your best to reassure yourself when they happen again that the symptoms will pass shortly. Remind yourself of all those times that you didn't pass out or die and were fine just 10 minutes later. This time should be no different, so make sure you are aware of that fact.

It's fairly common sense, but it should be said that you should avoid doing important things while going through a panic attack. If you're driving, for instance, you should most definitely pull over and wait it out. Otherwise, you wouldn't only be risking your life and that of others, but you'd just be making the attack worse, worrying about what can happen.

You should have a string of positive, reaffirming statements at the ready for when panic attacks occur. These statements are the ones you will be using on yourself to change your mindset into a positive one and get through the ordeal easier. The first thing you should remind yourself of is that your panic attacks aren't deadly. Remind yourself of facts such as that your panic attack is just a culmination of anxiety and that it is irrational – that there is nothing to be afraid of.

But that doesn't mean you should obsess over the panic, far from it. As is always the case with anxiety-related problems, distractions and a shift of focus can do wonders. There are many ways in which you can achieve this change in focus, but three come to mind first. For one, you can keep handy some pleasant reminder of positive things, such as a picture of something or someone dear to you. You can also try to visualize being somewhere else. You should try to think of a place that you love dearly, which particularly relaxes you, and try to imagine yourself being there, completely tranquil. Last but not least, it's always a good idea to try and make yourself laugh, at least on the inside.

With a little bit of creativity, the human mind can find the humor in any situation, no matter how hopeless things might seem. And remember, with your panic attacks and anxiety, things probably *aren't* hopeless to begin with, they seem that way in your exaggerated perception. For instance, if you are in a highly social situation, and you feel that a particular person is triggering your anxiety or panic, try to think of that person in a comical or humiliating situation. You will find that it's very easy to do this to people in your head, and it's a great way of making folks seem less menacing, especially if they are authority figures of some kind. Just make sure you don't laugh out loud at your boss or someone like that if it's not appropriate.

Of course, some medications treat symptoms of panic attacks and, since a doctor can diagnose both panic attacks and panic disorders, obtaining a prescription shouldn't be too difficult if you need it. Do keep in mind, however, that such medications are only short-term solutions and are best used in conjunction with other forms of therapy, such as counseling.

Long-Term Solutions

If you do have a full-blown panic disorder, you shouldn't refrain from seeking professional help. Of course, as always, there are certain home remedies, but the problem can sometimes be too big to solve on your own. As we just mentioned above, there are therapies you can greatly benefit from if your panic attacks are severe and you see no improvement on the horizon even with everything we have covered thus far.

Talking to a psychiatrist can and should be about much more than just getting a prescription and going about your way, popping pills. Cognitive-behavioral therapy, for instance, has demonstrated considerable results in these fields for years and even decades. With a personal therapist or counselor, you can take your time exploring the causes of your problem and all your other highly personal issues. This can help you plot the best possible approach to tackle the problem. The whole idea behind cognitive behavioral therapy is to rewire the way you think and use the power of your mind to beat the problem. Medication may or may not be used, depending on the individual approach.

In essence, many of the long-term solutions for panic disorders will be very similar to the approach to plain old social anxiety. Either as a part of your therapy or off your own accord, you can also try to incorporate various forms of meditation or yoga. Simple breathing meditation can be of use, but you can also try mindfulness. The nature of these exercises is such that they might fare particularly well when it comes to breaking that momentary hold that your panic has over you at a given time.

Meditation is something you can learn from trained instructors, but simpler techniques can also be learned online. Don't be dissuaded because you think it's something complicated and highly spiritual because it doesn't have to be. Meditative breathing exercises, for instance, consist of what we mentioned earlier plus a strong mental focus on the breathing process to push all other thoughts out of your head.

This is also essentially entry-level mindfulness, which is a technique that focuses on making you more present and grounded in the moment. The idea is to practice the control you have over your thoughts by focusing on and observing these processes in your head as neutrally as possible. Still, mindfulness is a broad range of exercises and meditations that some people use to achieve incredible results, so it might be worth looking into for you as well.

Yoga is another method that many people use to combat stress, anxiety, depression, and a plethora of other problems, including panic disorders. You can take up beginner-level Yoga on your own, just like meditation, by looking up a few techniques and exercises online, for instance. However, the best results will probably come from Yoga classes through group sessions or with a personal trainer. Yoga is about striking a balance between mind and body while also keeping both healthy and in shape. More often than not, this is exactly what anxious, stressed-out people need.

Something else to focus on in the long term is attaining a better, deeper understanding of your disorder. Whether it happens only in social situations or in multiple areas of your life, the important thing is to learn all of your triggers and make your outbursts as predictable as you possibly can. Remember, you're not learning these triggers so that you could run away and hide but prepare yourself and manage your reactions better.

There are many lifestyle changes you can introduce as a way of reducing either the severity or the frequency of your panic attacks, or both. Stress is a major contributor to panic disorders. Money problems, a stressful work environment, problems at home, and a million other life circumstances can cause immense stress, so you should do your best to reduce this bad influence as much as possible.

Overall, panic attacks are not to be taken lightly. Most of the methods used to treat anxiety will also work to reduce panic attacks, so stick to your program and keep working toward getting better. Don't forget, however, that extreme cases of panic disorders can be potentially life-threatening both to you and those around you, so you should know when to seek help.

If you have been at it for months, using everything we've covered here, and you see absolutely zero results, then it might be a good idea to pay a visit to your doctor who might recommend a psychiatrist. Remember, even if you are committed to beating your social anxiety on your own, it's a good idea to go to professionals, at least for diagnosis. This will help you learn a lot about your problem, and it certainly won't hurt. The more you understand your condition, the better.

Conclusion

In the end, it can be said that social anxiety is a problem with the potential to deprive your life of all that is good. Beating this disorder is a truly liberating experience that will make you feel reborn and like you can finally breathe again. Social anxiety is a burden that you carry due to no fault of your own, to no benefit, and for no good reason at all.

Being stressed out all the time expends valuable energy that can be used elsewhere and to meaningful ends. With social anxiety, you are spending your energy on irrationally stressing over meaningless things when you could be focusing on self-improvement and fulfilling hobbies, for instance. The sooner you get started on your journey toward recovery, the sooner you will be able to reassert yourself and get more out of life.

In this book, we have gone over the areas that you have to improve and practice to alleviate your social anxiety. You have learned about confidence, interaction, assertiveness, managing your fears, and much else. Remember the many situations that we have discussed, such as meetings, interviews, and presentations.

While these situations might be different, they will generally make you feel the same kind of dread, with the difference being merely a matter of degree. That's why improving your control in just one of those situations can have at least a mild positive effect on your level of anxiety in general.

It is a good idea to start small and simple. You can try to apply the simplest of the tips first and focus on improving your performance in those social situations that are the easiest for you. When trying to test your progress, don't just throw yourself into your nightmare scenario right away because you might start to panic and then end up discouraged.

Furthermore, you shouldn't forget the value of friends and family if you have them. You can always try to talk to them about your problems and look for support. You might find that just allowing another, trustworthy person to know about your troubles can make you feel better. Maybe you will also end up with some valuable, highly personalized advice that only your loved ones know how to give you.

The information you have gathered in this book will help you improve in those areas that reflect on your social anxiety, thus generally alleviating the problem indirectly. However, in a minority of cases, social anxiety can be incredibly intense and severe, requiring therapy. The first line of defense in treating social anxiety disorder is usually cognitive behavioral therapy (CBT), which consists of counseling and other drug-free approaches.

In a way, this book itself is a cognitive behavioral therapy approach as it seeks to alter your thought patterns, lifestyle choices, and other things that might be contributing to social anxiety. In those severe cases, however, people might require a committed, individual approach from a therapist or psychiatrist. Counseling and similar therapy have been proven to be very successful in combating social anxiety, even in support groups. You must understand is that there is no shame in seeking help. The quality of your future life might depend on it.

The most important thing to understand, however, is that your social anxiety disorder is treatable, no matter how helpless you might feel at this time. Keep in mind that social anxiety is an illness that wants you to accommodate it, though, which is the worst thing you could do. Do not let yourself cede ground to your illness and don't let it conquer more and more of your life. If it tells you not to go to that job interview or out with your friends, don't listen to it. Instead, remember what you have learned here and tackle the problem head-on and right away.

It's also worth pointing out that certain prescribed medications have been shown to help with the treatment of social anxiety. These tend to be in the classes of antidepressants, anti-anxiety drugs, and various other medications, particularly those that work to rebalance the chemical levels in your brain. As is often the case with these things, the best possible outcome is to get better without relying on drugs.

However, on rare occasions, that might not be possible. In moderation and with strict control, prescription drugs can certainly be a help. The important thing is to thoroughly consult with a psychiatrist and combine the drugs with CBT as part of a well-structured plan of therapy. You must stick to the program and never self-medicate or rely on any substances on your own, whether they are legal, illegal, or prescribed.

It can certainly be tempting, though. Alcohol, for example, is known as the social lubricant for a reason. It can inhibit your fear and anxiety and help you open up, but the potential to lose control both in the situation and in the long run is too high of a risk. Alcohol is one of the most common pitfalls and traps along the road for people suffering from all kinds of anxiety disorders, not just SAD.

All in all, your journey toward recovery will unveil many things to you and help you chart your path going forward. What matters is that you embark on that journey as soon as possible, and everything you've learned here will certainly help in that regard.

At the very least, you will feel better and learn to manage your anxious outbreaks through these techniques and tips. Still, as important as it is to manage the symptoms, you will have to address the underlying causes sooner or later and treat the illness. And if you're positive that you can't do that on your own, don't forget that there is plenty of help out there waiting just for people like you. It matters not if you happen to be friendless or far away from your family at this time – you are not beyond help. Let that be your first crucial realization, the building block upon which you will build the rest of your staircase toward recovery.

Good Fortune!

Resources

Intro

https://socialphobia.org/social-anxiety-disorder-definition-symptoms-treatment-therapy-medications-insight-prognosis

https://abcnews.go.com/Health/Healthday/story?id=4621523&page=1

https://adaa.org/about-adaa/press-room/facts-statistics

https://www.huffpost.com/entry/social-anxiety-by-the-numbers_n_5acb5934e4b09d0a1195aa91?guccounter=1&guce_referrer=aHR0cHM6Ly93d3cuZ29vZ2xlLmNvbS8&guce_referrer_sig=AQAAAHsLM6bouugO6KYh9zZU_5_IDSYiZ_9kEud3Yefgy6OFLtN0JWJxNkZFybJu_ohJdw4iJwmWUIOFbLj6qxaBOY0V5BLaDk6ZGE-7zNnzP8-fPiEytZFiDRF3z03C7kyJkk9PnW7fFqds4Opri-nKwdzkVbMxLOtCRLaLu6GJ4Pgl

https://www.nimh.nih.gov/health/statistics/social-anxiety-disorder.shtml

https://www.ajmc.com/journals/supplement/20
05/2005-10-vol11-n12suppl/oct05-2158ps344-
s353

Chapter One

https://www.webmd.com/anxiety-
panic/guide/mental-health-social-anxiety-
disorder#1

https://adaa.org/understanding-anxiety/social-
anxiety-disorder

https://www.anxietyuk.org.uk/anxiety-
type/social-anxiety/

https://www.verywellmind.com/coping-with-
social-anxiety-disorder-3024836

https://www.psycom.net/social-anxiety-test/

https://socialanxietyinstitute.org/social-anxiety-
and-aspergers-differences

Chapter 2

https://shynesssocialanxiety.com/heres-why-
you-cant-fake-confidence-if-you-have-social-
anxiety/

https://thoughtcatalog.com/adam-
rockman/2017/06/5-techniques-to-build-your-
confidence-and-beat-social-anxiety/

https://www.psychologytoday.com/us/articles/2
00703/confidence-stepping-out

http://www.hartsteinpsychological.com/reduce-
social-anxiety-increase-self-confidence

https://www.improvementzone.co.uk/project-
view/build-confidence-ease-social-anxiety/

https://talkitover.in/self/how-to-overcome-
social-anxiety-and-build-confidence

http://allwithinthemind.co.uk/common-
problems/social-anxiety-low-self-confidence/

https://www.psychologytoday.com/gb/blog/shyn
ess-is-nice/201812/5-reasons-people-have-low-
self-confidence

Chapter 3

https://www.verywellmind.com/talk-people-
social-anxiety-disorder-3024390

https://anxietycanada.com/articles/effective-
communication-improving-your-social-skills/

https://nationalsocialanxietycenter.com/2017/11
/15/social-anxiety-small-talk-nuts-bolts-making-
conversation/

https://www.healthcentral.com/article/conversa
tional-skills-for-the-socially-anxious

http://overcomingsocialanxiety.com/8-steps-to-making-smalltalk/

https://www.psychbytes.com/overcoming-social-anxiety-improving-your-conversation-skills/

https://www.social-anxiety-solutions.com/conversation-skills/

Chapter 4

https://www.psychologytoday.com/gb/blog/shyness-is-nice/201305/must-have-coping-strategies-social-anxiety

https://www.verywellmind.com/managing-social-anxiety-disorder-at-work-3024812

https://mellowed.com/social-anxiety-at-work/

http://overcomingsocialanxiety.com/how-to-manage-social-anxiety-at-work/

https://www.psycom.net/10-ways-manage-anxiety-work

https://www.bustle.com/p/how-to-manage-social-anxiety-at-work-9775244

https://themighty.com/2017/05/how-to-manage-social-anxiety-at-work/

Chapter 5

https://www.verywellmind.com/anxiety-in-meetings-3024310 ·

https://psychcentral.com/blog/5-ways-to-banish-anxiety-and-speak-up-in-meetings-at-work/

https://www.huffpost.com/entry/end-anxiety-in-the-workplace-with-this-one-trick_b_9064024?guccounter=1&guce_referrer=aHR0cHM6Ly93d3cuZ29vZ2xlLmNvbS8&guce_referrer_sig=AQAAAKoOPXewEVZToIdWbOnUZRH2fR16JZve6eaxUl65ZwUl26xZItMIWmJQjoEqVa4adVMwPJz5yX82FiFAjqc_JXnSAcVl6Q3LVg0Y4cbZYfNn5_-f2LaZlKgsQJeXl7PqEL_kfC_hOODFLnPn4i144-sdwFr2HRFbNYvLGQq4r80Q

https://www.verywellmind.com/tips-cope-with-job-interview-anxiety-3024324

https://introvertdear.com/news/interview-socially-anxiety-introvert/

https://www.psychologytoday.com/us/blog/career-transitions/201503/10-ways-calm-your-interview-anxiety

https://www.verywellmind.com/tips-for-giving-a-speech-3024402

http://overcomingsocialanxiety.com/courage-to-give-a-speech/

https://www.briantracy.com/blog/public-speaking/27-useful-tips-to-overcome-your-fear-of-public-speaking/

Chapter 6

https://www.beyondblue.org.au/get-support/online-forums/employment-and-workplaces/starting-a-new-job-and-terrified-of-panic

https://www.gq-magazine.co.uk/article/the-gq-therapist-how-to-handle-new-job-anxiety

https://www.reed.co.uk/career-advice/how-to-stop-feeling-nervous-about-starting-a-new-job/

https://www.fastcompany.com/90211103/what-to-do-when-you-feel-like-you-dont-fit-in-at-work

https://www.verywellmind.com/tips-for-telling-your-employer-that-you-have-sad-3024811

http://overcomingsocialanxiety.com/help-my-boss-scares-me/

https://www.themuse.com/advice/how-to-get-over-your-fear-of-your-boss

https://medium.com/brilliantforge/how-to-navigate-the-social-anxiety-minefield-of-work-15c87e182ae2

https://shynesssocialanxiety.com/dealing-with-difficult-people-when-you-have-social-anxiety/

https://www.businessinsider.com/9-useful-strategies-to-dealing-with-difficult-people-at-work-2011-6?r=US&IR=T

https://www.thebalancecareers.com/dealing-with-difficult-people-at-work-1917903

Chapter 7

https://www.forbes.com/sites/melodywilding/2016/08/01/the-one-rule-overachievers-need-to-stop-worrying-about-work-mistakes/#23ef04407364

https://www.psychologytoday.com/us/blog/fighting-fear/201402/making-terrible-mistakes-work

https://www.verywellmind.com/how-do-i-maintain-good-eye-contact-3024392

http://www.calmandcourageous.com/importance-eye-contact-reducing-social-anxiety/

https://themighty.com/2016/07/how-active-listening-can-help-ease-social-anxiety/

https://blogs.psychcentral.com/relationships-balance/2016/06/12/social-anxiety-the-dreaded-conversation/

https://www.makeuseof.com/tag/simple-mind-hacks-remembering-peoples-names/

https://www.nytimes.com/2019/05/30/style/trouble-remembering-names.html

https://www.psychologytoday.com/intl/blog/in-practice/201801/four-mistakes-people-anxiety-make

Chapter 8

https://www.verywellmind.com/how-can-i-be-more-assertive-when-i-have-social-anxiety-3024311

https://www.aboutsocialanxiety.com/become-assertive/

https://freefromsocialanxiety.com/simple-mind-hack-achieve-assertiveness/

https://www.psychologytoday.com/us/blog/think-act-be/201801/5-benefits-asserting-your-needs-and-how-start-today

https://www.elitedaily.com/life/anxiety-taught-me-assertiveness/1482666

Chapter 9

https://www.verywellmind.com/how-to-make-friends-3024380

https://themighty.com/2017/06/social-anxiety-friends-what-to-know/

https://metro.co.uk/2018/03/02/5-ways-to-make-new-friends-when-you-have-social-anxiety-7332485/

https://hellogiggles.com/love-sex/friends/making-friends-social-anxiety/

https://thoughtcatalog.com/holly-riordan/2018/04/12-ways-your-friendships-are-different-when-you-have-anxiety/

https://www.psychologytoday.com/intl/blog/the-friendship-doctor/201010/when-anxiety-gets-in-the-way-friendship

https://anxiouslass.com/make-friends-social-anxiety/

https://freedomacademyhq.com/how-to-make-friends-with-social-anxiety/

https://www.helpguide.org/articles/relationships-communication/dealing-with-loneliness-and-shyness.htm

https://hellogiggles.com/love-sex/friends/8-ways-to-make-friends-when-you-have-anxiety/

https://welldoing.org/article/6-ways-to-nurture-your-friendships

http://goodlifezen.com/10-simple-ways-to-strengthen-friendships-for-a-lifetime-2/

Chapter 10

https://www.mind.org.uk/information-support/types-of-mental-health-problems/anxiety-and-panic-attacks/panic-attacks/?gclid=CjwKCAjwnrjrBRAMEiwAXsCc40tnJhFmQfTh0_djHEi7xjEUgqx1cfpbCBEnGBN5RQserH_6cXgDzhoCYcAQAvD_BwE#.XY1KxkYzZph

https://www.healthline.com/health/panic-attack-vs-anxiety-attack

https://www.webmd.com/anxiety-panic/guide/anxiety-attack-symptoms

https://www.priorygroup.com/blog/5-top-tips-for-coping-with-panic-attacks

https://www.medicalnewstoday.com/articles/321510.php

https://ibpf.org/article/9-tips-help-you-get-through-panic-attack

https://www.verywellmind.com/managing-panic-disorder-in-public-2584185

https://www.self.com/story/panic-attack-tips

https://www.anxietycoach.com/overcoming-panic-attacks.html

https://www.everydayhealth.com/anxiety/how-to-handle-panic-attacks.aspx

DON'T BE SAD!

9 798666 784256 9